“十三五”职业教育部委级规划教材

江苏高校品牌专业建设工程资助项目（PPZY2015C254）

纺织品外贸跟单
（双语）

朱　挺　王　可　主　编

陆晓波　马　倩　副主编

中国纺织出版社有限公司

内 容 提 要

　　本书是"十三五"职业教育部委级规划教材中的一种,采用中英双语编写,内容丰富,引用数据皆来自最近年份,借鉴性强。在编排上偏重于英文,只在每个章节以及关键要点给出中文对照。本书介绍了国内外纺织行业的发展现状、纺织品相关基础知识、合同相关知识以及纺织品检测知识,在此基础上,按订单操作的时间顺序详细介绍了纺织品外贸跟单的整个流程,包括样品跟单、质量跟单、数量跟单、包装跟单、运输跟单、保险跟单。本书在末尾收录了一些外贸跟单相关的参考资料。

　　本书适合高等职业教育阶段纺织服装、贸易相关专业师生参考及相关从业人员阅读。

图书在版编目(CIP)数据

　　纺织品外贸跟单:汉、英/朱挺,王可主编. --北京:中国纺织出版社有限公司,2020.8 (2023.1重印)
　　"十三五"职业教育部委级规划教材
　　ISBN 978-7-5180-7447-1

　　Ⅰ.①纺…　Ⅱ.①朱…　②王…　Ⅲ.①纺织品—市场营销学—高等职业教育—教材—汉、英　Ⅳ.①F768.3

　　中国版本图书馆 CIP 数据核字(2020)第 085147 号

责任编辑:符　芬　　责任校对:寇晨晨　　责任印制:何　建

中国纺织出版社有限公司出版发行
地址:北京市朝阳区百子湾东里 A407 号楼　邮政编码:100124
销售电话:010—67004422　传真:010—87155801
http://www.c-textilep.com
中国纺织出版社天猫旗舰店
官方微博 http://weibo.com/2119887771
三河市宏盛印务有限公司印刷　　各地新华书店经销
2020 年 8 月第 1 版　　2023 年 1 月第 4 次印刷
开本:787×1092　1/16　印张:10.25
字数:210 千字　定价:52.00 元

| 前 言 |

我国自加入世界贸易组织以来,纺织服装行业对外出口量迅猛增长,不仅为国家外汇储备做出了巨大贡献,也解决了大量人口就业问题。日渐频繁的对外贸易活动不仅促进了经济的迅猛发展,也创造了新的职业与岗位需求,为有志于在对外贸易领域大展才华的求职者提供了更加广阔的空间,外贸跟单员就是众多兴起的新岗位之一,纺织品外贸跟单员是指在进出口贸易合同签订后,依据外贸合同或信用证,对货物的样品、生产、包装、运输、保险等部分或全部业务环节进行跟踪或操作,协助贸易合同履行的外贸业务人员。

当前,大部分院校纺织专业都开设了外贸跟单类课程,以培养学生从事纺织品进出口业务的能力,但由于外贸跟单工作的涉外性特点,要求学生具备良好的英语水平并掌握大量的纺织行业专业术语,以便毕业生更好地适应未来相应岗位的工作,因此,在该课程上开展双语教学,可以更好地帮助学生在掌握纺织品跟单业务流程的基础上,实现相应语言技能的提升。但目前在相关课程的教学上基本全部使用中文教材,全英文或中英双语教材十分稀缺,本书的编写就是基于这样的市场需要。

《纺织品外贸跟单(双语)》由江苏盐城工业职业技术学院纺织服装学院多名教师合作编写,历时两年,查阅了大量文献资料并经历了多次修改。本书的编写人员长期在一线岗位上从事纺织品外贸跟单及相关课程的教学,具有丰富的教学经验,同时,也具有数年纺织品出口企业工作经历,熟悉出口流程,能够独立操作出口订单,在从教期间多次参加大型纺织品展会,承担语言翻译任务,这些企业实践经历为本书的编写提供了很多经验借鉴。

本教材在内容上涵盖了纺织品外贸跟单的各个环节,共分十个章节,包括:纺织品国际市场概述、纺织基本知识、签订合同、样品跟单、质量跟单、货物数量跟单、包装跟单、货物运输跟单、运输保险跟单和纺织品检验,在内容选取上注重贴近企业实践。本书由朱挺、王可担任主编,陆晓波、马倩担任副主编,其中朱挺编写第一、第三、第九、第十章,马倩编写第二章,王可编写第四、第七章,陆晓波编写第五、第六章,王曙东编写第八章,此外,江苏盐城工业职业技术学院赵磊也对本书部分章节提供了宝贵的资料,本书由陈宏武、刘华、周彬担任主审。

本书在编写过程中得到了职业教育"现代纺织技术"专业国家教学资源库建设子项目(FZZYK2015-22-7)、江苏高校品牌专业建设工程(PPZY2015C254)、江苏省高等职业教育产教深度融合实训平台和江苏省高校青蓝工程、2020 年度江苏省高校"青蓝工程"中青年学术带头人(苏教师函[2020]10 号)等项目的资助,也得到了江苏工程职业技术学院和全国纺织服装职业教育教学指导委员会等的支持,在此一并表示感谢。

由于时间紧、任务重,编写人员水平有限,书中存在错误和疏漏之处在所难免,恳请专家与同行批评指正。

编　者
2020 年 3 月

Contents 目录

Chapter Four　Smaple Management

Chapter Five　Quality of Commodity

Chapter Six　Quantity of Goods

Chapter Seven　Packing of Goods

Chapter One　Overview of Textile Business in Global Market

第一章　纺织品国际市场概述

进入 21 世纪以来,伴随经济全球化发展,纺织服装业正在从劳动密集型向技术密集型转变,发达国家的资金、技术和发展中国家的劳动力比较优势都在不断改变世界纺织品的生产和贸易格局。与此同时,纺织品的应用领域也开始发生变化。过去,绝大多数纺织品主要是用于服装的生产,而随着技术的发展,纺织品的种类逐渐增多,纺织品的应用领域也开始向装饰用和产业用扩展。科技含量的增加使得纺织品行业更倾向于技术密集型,影响纺织服装业竞争力的关键因素也不再主要是劳动力,而开始转向科技水平。

Section One　Global Textile Business Markets

第一节　全球纺织品市场

当今,纺织服装业的世界生产格局和贸易格局已经发生了显著变化。世界纺织服装业的生产中心已从发达国家转移到发展中国家。生产地与消费地的分离使纺织品和服装的国际贸易不断增加。目前,中国、欧盟和印度仍然是世界上主要的三大纺织品出口国(地区)。我国在纺织服装产业链、行业规模、生产配套能力等方面都达到了较好的水平,纺织行业的市场化、国际化程度较高。纺织业是印度历史最久、规模最大的行业,是印度的支柱产业。印度的产棉量、黄麻产量、丝绸产量、织机数量、纱线产量、合成纤维产量在全球排名均名列前茅,不容小觑。

1.World Textile Markets Overview 世界纺织市场概述

The world experienced the major changeover in the textile business with British industrial revolution, where the British took the technology to India etc. So the developed countries became the origin of technology while the developing countries moved towards being the manufacturing hubs due to the abundant manpower.

Textile industry is an important pillar industry in China. Since 1994, China has been the biggest export country of textile clothing in the world. With first-class technology and stronger competitiveness of the world, textile industry has become one of the most important manufacture industries of China. Fig1.1 shows a busy Chinese port.

The global textile market was valued at approximately USD858 billion in 2018 and is expected to generate around USD1,207 billion by 2025. The success of the modern industry of world textiles is dependent largely upon continuing major investment in innovation and invention. The reason which forces the textile business to the promotion is the increasing share of technical textiles.

Globally, the technical textiles contribute to about 27% of the world textile industry, in some of the western countries its share is even 50%. The global technical textile market is projected to grow at a compound annual growtl rate （CAGR） of 5.16% to reach USD334.938 billion by 2025.

Fig 1.1　A Busy Chinese Port

According to the *World Trade Statistical Review* 2019 released by the World Trade Organization （WTO）, China, European Union （EU28）, and India remained the world′s top three exporters of textiles in 2018. Altogether, these top three accounted for 66.9% of world textile exports in 2018. China, the European Union （EU28）, Bangladesh, and Vietnam unshakably remained the world′s top four largest apparel exporters in 2018. Altogether, these top four accounted for as much as 72.3% of world market shares in 2018. The European Union （EU28）, the United States, and China were the top three largest importers of textiles in 2018, accounting for 37.5% of the world′s total textile imports that year. Affected by consumers′ purchasing power （often measured by gross domestic product–GDP per capita） and size of the population, the European Union, the United States, and Japan remained the world′s top three importers of apparel in 2018. Altogether, these top three absorbed 61.5% of world apparel in 2018.

Asia is the leader in terms of the installed capacity of textile machinery, 86% of short–staple spindles, 45% of long staple spindles, 55% of rotor spinning machines, 73% of shuttleless looms and 85% of shuttle looms are installed in Asia alone. China, India, Pakistan, Indonesia and Thailand are among the leaders in terms of this installed capacity. China is a consistent leading exporter in the global textile market whereas India, Italy, Germany, Ban-

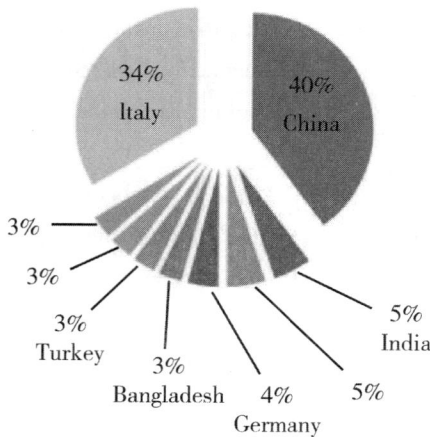

Fig 1.2　Major Exporters in Global Textile Exports

gladesh are other leading countries. Fig 1.2 shows the distribution map of major exporters in global textile exports.

2.Leading Exporters in Global Textiles 世界主要纺织出口国

(1)Overview of Chinese Textile & Apparel Industry

In China, six sub-industries of the textile industry include cotton, chemical fiber textile and printing & dyeing finishing industry, wool textile and dyeing finishing industry, linen textile, silk textile and finishing industry, finished textile product manufacturing as well as knitted and woven product industry.

As a traditional advantage industry, textile industry plays an important role in national economy. China is the world's largest textile producer and exporter. The output volume of China textile industry accounts for more than half of the global one. The processing capacity and export value of textile fiber account for a higher proportion in the world. The market international share exceeds one third of the world.

It is predicted that in the next 3-5 years, China textile industry in possess of perfect industry chain and large domestic market will continue to maintain a certain advantage in the world. However, in the longer run, the costs of China textile industry rise so fast that the production capacity of the textile industry will continue to transfer overseas, which will undermine the overall advantages of China textile industry chain.

(2)Overview of Indian Textile & Apparel Industry

Indian textile industry is one of the leading textile industries in the world. Indian textile industry largely depends upon the textile manufacturing and export. It also plays a major role in the economy of the country. India earns about 27% of its total foreign exchange through textile exports. Further, the textile industry of India also contributes nearly 14% of the total industrial production of the country. It also contributes around 3% to the GDP of the country.

Indian textile industry can be divided into several segments, some of whichcan be listed as below: cotton textiles, silk textiles, woolen textiles, readymade garments, hand-crafted textiles, jute and coir.

(3) Leading Exporters in Global Textile Machinery Exports

The textile industry is developing at a high speed, especially after the abolishment of global quota scheme. The textile machinery, which is an essential sector for the production chain, has also experienced some revolution with a lot of new technologies. The range of textile machinery used in the sector is, therefore, large. More than 80 tariff lines cover the international trade of textile machinery and spare parts which are used directly in manufacturing of textiles and clothing products.

The textile machinery manufacturing hubs like China, Germany, Italy, Switzerland and India have already jumped in gigantic competition to craft and bid best technologies in textile machineries.

a. China, the biggest machinery manufacturer in the global textile arena

The Chinese textile manufacturers are developing some of the best answers intechnical aspects of textile industry, along with very competitive prices. China-made textile machinery and equipment account for 80 percent of domestic textile machinery market.

China is not only exporter of textile machinery but also a potential importer of textile machinery. The potential import markets for textile machineries were Chinese provinces like Jiangsu, Zhejiang and Guangdong, which accounted for roughly 71% of the Chinese overall textile machinery imports.

b. Germany provides technology support to the textile machinery

Germany has jumped out as a crucial manufacturer of textile machinery and has secured its place by the 5th rank worldwide in machinery export. The key strengths of German machinery manufacturers become obvious if one considers the entire life cycle of a machine. During the entire lifetime of a machine, the investment costs represent only about 10 to 50 per cent of the overall costs.

German textile machinery is characterized by its high quality and customer-specific production. The trend setting players in the German textile machinery industry have never stopped to explore new application fields which provide them with great opportunities.

c. Italian textile machinery industry grows strongly

Italian textile machinery industrial sector is one of the foremost machinery manufacturers comprising around 300 companies (employing roughly 12,400 people) and producing machinery for an overall value of USD3.41 billion per year, with exports amounting to 80% of total sales.

Exports were always the driving force behind the sectors growth in Italy. The enthusiasm of major textile markets, combined with the capability of Italian machinery manufacturers to assert them on a global scale, contributed to sustained growth in exports.

d. The textile machinery, a strong demand in the whole world

Textile machinery manufacturing is an essential part for the production chain, which becomes a strong demand in the world. Investment in this sector needs to be encouraged to decrease dependence on imports and ultimately leads to export of notonly textiles and clothing products but machinery and spares parts as well. Price, flexibility and versatility comprise the determining factors for new equipment purchases. As such, the market is witnessing emergence of more efficient machines, at competitive prices, thanks to rapid technological advances in the textile machinery industry. End-users are increasingly seeking complete automation solutions with enhanced flexibility that can be availed at reasonable costs.

Section Two   Future Prospect in Textile
第二节　纺织业未来展望

受全球经济增长的推动,人们可支配收入稳步提升,进而推动全球纺织市场规模不断壮大,据统计,全球服装零售市场规模年均复合增长率为 3.87%,2018 年服装零售总额达 14000 亿美元。

未来的纺织品,将继续向着功能化、智能化的方向发展,将来可能看到 3D 打印服装、NFC 交互式服装、VR 模特、变色面料、自愈面料等产品成为现实。不断地提升我们的生活水平。

1.The Growth of Regional Markets 区域市场的增长

Countries like China, India, Russia and Brazil are emerging as apparelretail markets and will form significant alternate markets to EU, USA, and Japan. Tab 1.1 shows the regional apparel markets growth. In years China and India will have huge growing markets. The growth of apparel market is stagnating in the traditional consuming hubs of EU, USA, and Japan. As the per capita spend on apparel is more in these countries, markets need importing of apparels so it makes more chances for growing apparel markets for trading.

Tab 1.1   Regional Apparel Markets Growth

Region	2013 (in billion USD)	2025 (in billion USD)	CAGR
EU	355	440	2%
USA	230	285	2%
China	165	540	10%
Japan	110	150	2%
Brazil	60	100	5%
India	46	200	12%
Russia	45	105	8%
Canada	30	50	4%
Australia	25	45	5%
Rest of the world	80	195	8%
Total	1146	2110	5%

The current global apparel market is estimated at approximately USD1.15 trillion which forms nearly 1.8% of the world GDP. Almost 75% of this market is concentrated in EU, USA, China and Japan. The next largest markets are Brazil, India, Russia, Canada, and Australia, in descending order with a share of approximately 18%. Tab 1.2 shows the regional apparel market size.

Tab 1.2   Regional Apparel Market Size

Size No.	Region	Size (in million USD)
1	EU	355
2	US	230
3	China	165
4	Japan	110

Continued

Size No.	Region	Size (in million USD)
5	Brazil	60
6	India	46
7	Russia	45
8	Canada	30
9	Australia	25
10	Rest world	80
Total		1146

Within the top markets, there is a major distinction between developed countries and the emerging ones in terms of per capita spend on apparel. Fig 1.3 shows the per capita spend on apparel in different regions. The lowest per capita spend on apparel among these markets is India (USD37). Australian per capita spend on apparel is the highest one with USD1131.

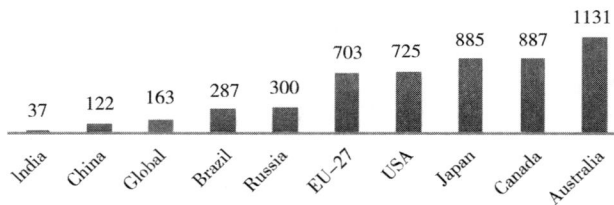

Fig 1.3　Per Capita Spend on Apparel (in USD)

There is a positive correlation between consumer's spending on various categories and the economic stature of each country. In less developed economies, consumer's spending is highest on food followed by clothing, housing, and other items. In developed economies, as the consumer's disposable income increases, the share of basic categories such as apparel reduces, whereas the share of new categories like entertainment, recreation, consumer durable, travel etc. increases.

Based on this fact, it is expected that the per capita spends on apparel will grow at a faster rate than the economy in Brazil, Russia, India, and China; whereas it will be slower or at par with the economic growth in developed markets over next few years.

2.Possible Technologies Ready to Change Fashion 可能改变时尚的未来新技术

Far from futuristic fantasy, we take a look at five technologies being trialled right now with the potential to change the world of fashion in ways we've never seen before.

（1）3D-printed Clothing

Proberly, you've seen at least one example of 3D printing in fashion, and it fell somewhere between a prop from Battlestar Galactica and one of those spiderwebs woven on acid. While there's been some jaw-dropping exploration of this technology over the years, there's been a tendency for early adopters to let their imaginations run wild, with little thought for how their work might be integrated into a less ostentatious wardrobe one day.

All that has changed in the past 12 months, as more grounded uses of 3D printing have emerged from a handful of established, reputable brands. While Nike's use of the technology to help them refine and perfect performance athletic footwear might seem like an obvious direction, Pringle of Scotland's surprise deployment of 3D printing in their Fall/Winter 2014 knitwear collection showed the world just how effectively traditional and hyper-modern manufacturing processes can combine in one remarkably normal end-product. This is arguably a far better indication of where the future for such processes lie. "Fingertrap Dress" or the work of hyper-conceptual designers like Iris van Herpen.

（2）NFC Interactive Clothing

For those unfamiliar with the acronym, NFC (or near field communication) is already changing the area of retail. It's the technology behind wireless payment, and its uses in stores and display advertising allow companies to offer targeted promotions and marketing opportunities to anyone inclined to waft their smartphone over one of the little chips. In the future, the advertising industry hopes to extend this to unsolicited push notifications, pinpointing shoppers on certain streets or even within particular aisles of a store using NFC "beacons" dotted strategically around the place.

If that sounds worryingly invasive to you, you're not alone, and concerns have been raised over the technology's impact on personal privacy. But there's yet another way NFC could still break into everyday life. Imagine walking into a store, finding something you like the look of, swiping your phone over the tag and being instantly shown a lookbook of ideas for how to style that item. The chip could also provide further information about the materials used in the garment's construction, its long-term care instructions or details of any in-store promotional offers. Perhaps you're just browsing, but want to keep a record of the items you liked while you wait for payday, all of that would be possible with the help of NFC.

（3）VR Models

While it might seem like certain celebrity models are everywhere you look, the fact is they (like all of us) are limited to one physical place at a time. They're only human, after all. But what if we told you the days of the human model were numbered, and that it was possible for brands to showcase their wares as they would appear in real life, all over the world, without the need for real people to wear them at all?

Fashion brands have been designing clothing using 3D rendering software for some time now, as it allows them to tweak and refine aspects of the cut and fit quickly, with minimal cost. More recently, scientists at the UK's Manchester Metropolitan University have been experimenting with a combination of 3D body scanners (the kind used in the most technical end of the fashion industry) and Hollywood-style motion-capture equipment to create ultra-realistic, near-flawless digital recreations of the human body. With a little programming, these digital avatars can be "dressed" in whatever clothing the programmers desire, resulting in a computer-generated fashion model with all the movement and appearances of the real thing.

(4) Color-changing Fabrics

While parts of the fashion world obsess over an ever-changing parade of "This Season's Hottest Color," a small group of pioneers are perfecting the means to rewrite the spectrum entirely. A far cry from the gimmicky heat-sensitive Hypercolor T-shirts of the 1990s, modern advances in photochromatic technology are throwing up some intriguing possibilities for the way we dress, and how our clothes themselves react to our environment.

What's most exciting about modern color-changing technology is that it's progressing from a number of different directions, each one built on entirely different scientific principles. The first, currently being explored by scientists at the University of Michigan, involves a membrane of tiny crystals that react differently when exposed to various wavelengths of light. As the light shines on a wafer-thin sheet of indium tin oxide, a charge is created that causes the crystals to change their formation, affecting the fabric's color and outward appearance. The U.S. military has already expressed interest in using this technology to develop active camouflage (much like that of a chameleon), but scientists working on the project have given no reason why it couldn't be adapted for the consumer marketplace as well.

(5) Self-healing Fabrics

You might think it's the stuff of *Terminator*, but self-healing fabrics are actually a part of our lives right now, and they're about to start multiplying. While rips and tears in any item of clothing are an annoyance, when it comes to waterproof garments the problem affects more than just looks. For this reason, researchers at Deakin University in Australia have been working on a fabric with superamphiphobic properties that can repair itself after damage and still keep liquids out.

Explained at length in the scientific journal *Applied Materials and Interfaces*, the basic principle behind the fabric is a special coating that, when damaged, melts at a very low temperature to seal the gap and normalize the waterproof properties. This also applies to the machine washing of clothes, which can prove a real obstacle when maintaining the performance of technical fabrics. During testing, the folks at Deakin found the fabric could stand up to 100 scratches with a razor blade before the waterproofing was seriously compromised, and over 200 wash cycles.

But that's not all. And, if that ever happens, it's safe to say you'll never look at your wardrobe the same way again.

Quiz 课后思考题

1. 请查阅 *World Trade Statistical Review* 2019,找出 2018 年全球纺织品和服装的出口额是多少? 其中,纺织品出口量最大的十个国家(地区)是哪些? 分别占多少份额?

2. 查阅资料,找出今年我国纺织品和服装市场规模、出口额以及占世界比重。

3. 近年来,面对劳动力成本优势逐渐丧失、原材料成本上升、国际贸易保护主义抬头等一系列因素,必须重新审视纺织业的出口问题,作为纺织从业人员,你有何想法和建议?

4. 谈谈你对纺织行业转型升级和产业转移的看法。

Chatpter Two　Basic Knowledge of Textile
第二章　纺织基本知识

　　在外贸跟单过程中,产品知识是业务能力的重要组成部分,是买卖双方交易的标的物,成为本行业的"内行"是做好跟单工作的前提。跟单员对产品各种相关知识了解得越多,就越能提高自信心,在面对客户的咨询时,就可以详细地告知各种产品的细节,为客户提供解决方案,让客户产生信任感。同时,当出现产品质量纠纷时,在与客户的交涉中就能够言之有物,展现良好的业务水平,有理有节地解决矛盾,维护公司利益。

　　优秀的纺织品外贸跟单员必须对纺织产品知识有比较深入的了解。本章将按照纺织品的生产工艺流程,分为纤维、纱线、面料三节分别介绍。

Section One　Textile Fibers
第一节　纺织纤维

　　目前,纺织工业中可用的纺织纤维很多,按照来源,纺织纤维可分为天然纤维和化学纤维。天然纤维包括植物纤维、动物纤维和矿物纤维,化学纤维包括再生纤维、合成纤维。

　　In textile, there are some important basic terms such as fiber, yarn, filament, fabric. See Fig 2.1. These terms are discussed below.

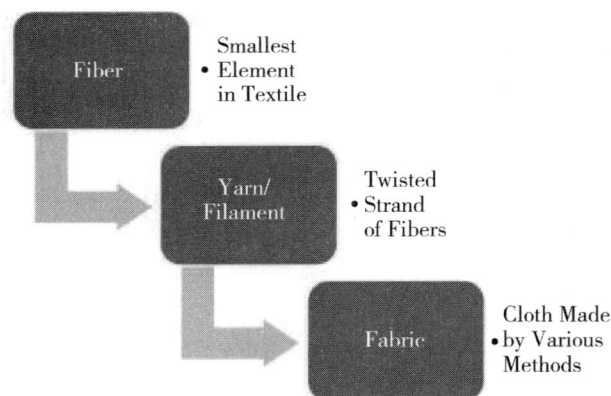

Fig 2.1　Textile Components

1.Overview of Textile Fibers 纺织纤维概述

　　The basic raw material of textile is fiber. Fiber is a textile material which is characterized by its various properties like length, fineness, colour, strength, etc. Fiber is the substance which is very small in diameter in relation to their length. Fibers may be natural or synthetic (man-made fibers).

Fiber is the material which is several hundred times longer than its thickness. Fiber is the basic component of any textile material. There are different types of fibers around us in daily use. Fibers with a short length are called as staple fibers, whereas fibers with long length are called as filaments. Fig 2.2 shows the classification of textile fibers.

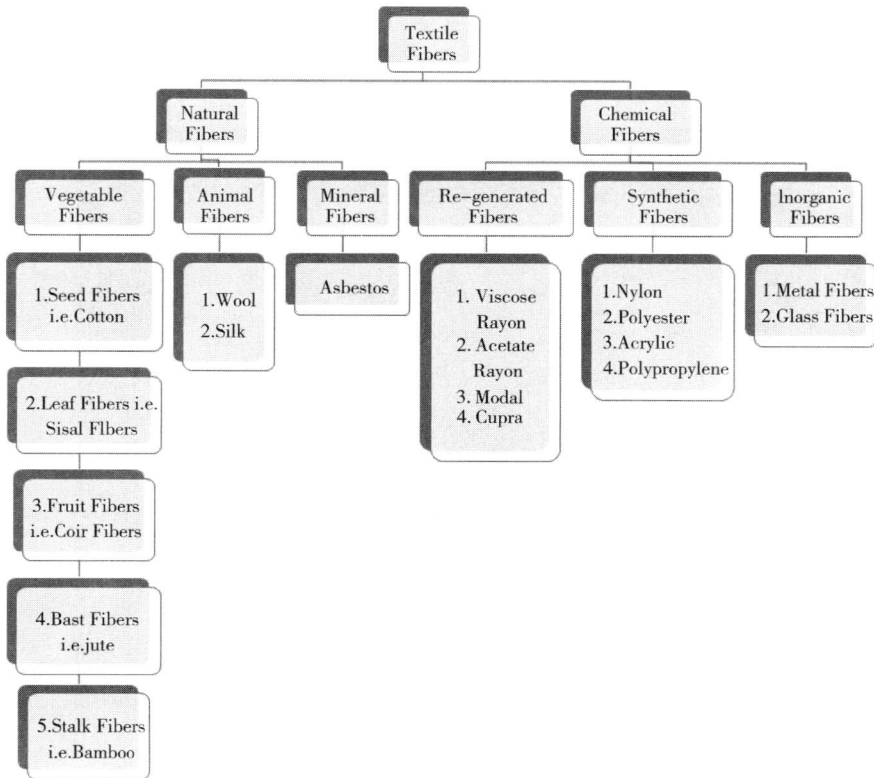

Fig 2.2   Textile Fiber Classification

Natural fibers are those which are obtained from natural sources such as cotton, jute (Vegetable Origin), wool, silk (Animal Origin), asbestos (Mineral Origin).

The various properties of these fibers depend on from which origin they are obtained. As the name itself indicates these fibers are made by man to obtain the various properties inherent in the fiber for the purpose of the particular application.

Synthetic fibers are manufactured by the process of polymerization of various monomers. Synthetic fibers are polyester, nylon, polypropylene, etc.

2.Natural Fibers 天然纤维

Fibers which are obtained from the natural origin directly or indirectly referred as natural fibers. Fibers obtained from the natural origin can be further sub-classified into three different categories, separately named vegetable fibers, animal fibers and mineral fibers, based on their different natural origins.

(1)Vegetable Fibers

These fibers are basically cellulosic fibers. Besides their use as textiles, these fibers are also used in the manufacturing of papers. Vegetable fibers are basically obtained from variousparts (organs) of the plants such as seeds, bast, leaf, fruit, stalk.

Seed fibers are obtained from seeds such as cotton, kapok. The cotton fibers are widely used for the apparel purpose, medical uses, and other textile applications. Fig 2.3 shows cotton, one of the most used seed fibers.

Fig. 2.3   Cotton in Blossom

Leaf fibers are obtained from leaves of plants such as pineapple, sisal, agave. Leaf fibers are used for marine ropes and cement reinforcement.

Fruit fibers are obtained from the fruit of the plant such as coir fiber (coconut fruit). These fibers are mainly used for manufacturing doormats, carpets.

Bast fibers are obtained from the bast surrounding to the stem of the plant. Such as jute, hemp, flax, ramie. These fibers have more strength, durability and do not get affected by moisture so that they are used for manufacturing durable yarns, fabrics, packaging material and paper.

Stalk fibers are extracted from stalks of the plant , such as straws of rice, wheat, and other crops. Bamboo and grass fiber is also included.

(2)Animal Fibers

The fibers obtained from animals are called as animal fibers. The fibers are mainly made up of protein molecules. The basic element of a protein molecule is carbon, nitrogen, hydrogen, oxygen.

Wool (hair fibers obtained from the animals) and silk fibers are common examples of animal fibers.

The fibers obtained from the **sheep** are referred as wool fibers, in the way the hair of the horse, camel, goat are also obtained as fiber. 90% of hair fibers are wool fibers used for various applications.

Silk is very delicate filament. It is obtained from silkworms. Silk formation takes place by the secretion of proteinous molecules in liquid form through the glands of the silkworm. It is located on the head of the worm. This liquid proteinous material gets converted into the solid filament. During this secretion process, the worm forms cocoons from which silk is extracted.

（3）Mineral Fibers

These are the inorganic materials shaped into fibers. Asbestos is the example of mineral fiber. These fibers are fireproof, resistance to acid so that these fibers mainly found in the industrial application.

3.Chemical Fibers 化学纤维

As the name itself indicates these textile fibers are made by mankind to meet the particular requirements. The chemical composition, structure, and properties are significantly modified during the manufacturing process.

Depending on the raw materials' these textile fibers can be further sub-classified into 3 categories: regenerated fibers, synthetic fibers, in-organic fibers.

（1）Regenerated Fibers

Regenerated synthetic textile fibers are also called as semi-synthetic fibers. These fibers are made up of naturally long chain polymer structure, which is modified and partially degraded by a chemical process to enable the polymerization reaction to form the fibers. Most of the semi-synthetic fibers are called cellulose regenerated fibers.

Examples: Viscose rayon, modal, cupra (rayon), bamboo viscose, tencell.

The cellulose required comes from various sources such as rayon from the tree wood, modal from the beech trees, seacell from seaweed. In the manufacturing process of these fibers, cellulose is fairly reduced to the pure viscose form and then foamed into the fiber form by extrusion through the spinnerets.

（2）Synthetic Fiber

Synthetic fibers are manufactured from the petrochemicals.

Examples: Polyester, nylon, acrylic, etc.

These fibers are formed by the polymerization of monomers. Once the polymer is formed, it can be formed into a filament by converting that polymer into fluid form and then extruding the molten or dissolved polymer through narrow holes to give filaments. To form the fiber from molten polymer it gets passed through the spinneret.

These fibers are generally very strong, fine and durable with very low moisture absorbency property so that these fibers are also called as hydrophobic fibers.

（3）In-Organic Fiber

These textile fibers are also called as metallic fibers. Metallic fibers are drawn from the ductile metals such as copper, gold, silver and can be extruded or deposited from more brittles such as nickel, aluminum and iron. From stainless steel also fibers can be formed.

These fibers are not that much widely used but these fibers have their special applications in technical textiles.

Section Two   Textile Yarn
第二节　纱线

目前,我国纺纱能力和产量位居世界第一,但是出口所占比例不大,大部分用于国内深加工。纱线从制成方法上可以分为两类:一类为长丝纱,是不需要经过纺纱过程而制成,如蚕丝、锦纶丝等;另一类为各种短纤维或中长纤维经过纺纱过程而制成的纱线。本节介绍常见的纺织用纱线。

1.Textile Yarn Overview 纱线概述

Yarn can be defined as a linear assembly of fibers or continuous filaments formed into a continuous strand with the required characteristics for textile. These textile characteristics include the good tensile strength and high flexibility so that it can be pliable and to be considered to a yarn, these yarns must be processable on conventional textile equipment and they must possess the visual and aesthetic characteristics which are usually associated with textile products.

The yarn is a continuous strand of fibers twisted together and with desirable strength. Fig 2.4 shows textile yarn in cone package.

Fig 2.4　Textile Yarn in Cone Package

The yarn is made up of staple fibers either natural or synthetic fiber. Yarn can be produced by various methods such as ring spinning, open end spinning, air jet spinning etc.

Whereas a monofilament is just one single filament (Fiber) that is usually not twisted. Filaments are made by grouping the single monofilament together and then twisting or air entangling. The filaments are made up of synthetic materials such as petrochemicals. There are some filaments manufactured from natural cellulose such as rayon, modal and lyocell. These kinds of filaments are called as regenerated filaments.

Combination yarns are made by plying the dissimilar components such as staple and continuous filament yarns. Yarns can be easily classified according to their physical properties. The classification of yarn is as given below.

2.Staple Yarns 短纤维纱

There are four different systems of manufacturing the staple yarn on the commercial level. These four systems are: the carded cotton yarn system, and the combed cotton yarn system, the worsted yarn system, and the woolen yarn system.

The yarn made from the staple fibers is known as staple yarn. The carded cotton and the combed cotton system are used to spin yarn from the short (up to 1 inch, 1 inch = 2.54cm) or long (2 - 3 inch) staple cotton or similar fibers. The woolen and the worsted system are used to spin yarn from the short (up to 2.5 inch) or long (up to 3.9 inch) staple fibers or similar fibers. Fig 2.5 shows the structure of the common cotton spun yarn.

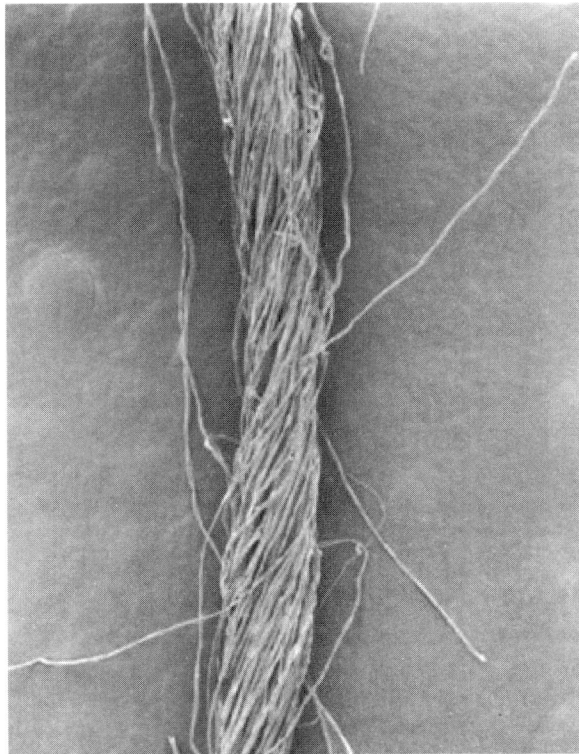

Fig 2.5   The Structure of the Common Cotton Spun Yarn

Chemical fibers are usually cut to a fiber length. The diameter and crimp are resembling that of cotton or wool for processing on this system. The fabrics made from staple yarn have good tactile properties such as a good handle, feel and excellent comfort along with the good aesthetic appearance.

3.Continuous Filament Yarn(连续)长丝纱

Before the manufacture of chemical fibers, silk was the only filament yarn. While manufacturing manmade filaments, a solution is forced through very fine holes of a spinneret, at which point the solution solidified by coagulation, evaporation or by cooling.

The number of holes in a spinneret determines the number of filaments. The size of hole and drawing (if any drawing) determine or affect the diameter of the filament. As soon as the individual filament solidifies, they are brought together with or without slight twist or entanglement to form the continuous filament yarn. Fig 2.6 shows the SEM image of 34 filament yarn.

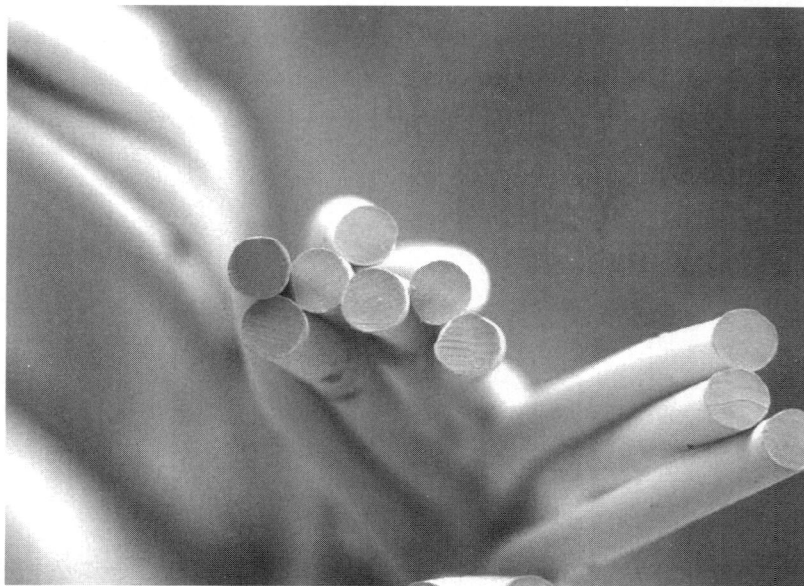

Fig 2.6   SEM Image of 34 Filament Yarn

The main advantage of chemical continuous filament yarns is that the physical and chemical properties of these yarns can be altered as per the end use requirement. But chemical continuous filaments are lack in their comfort properties, tactile properties, good covering properties and pleasing appearance in their untextured form.

Continuous filament yarns and the fabric made from it are much stronger and uniform than staple yarns and the fabric.

4.Novelty Yarns 新型纱线

Novelty yarns are also called as effect threads or effect yarns or fancy yarns. These yarns are mainly manufactured or designed for decorative purpose rather than functional purpose. Very rarely the entire fabric is composed of novelty yarns. Most of the novelty yarns are basically either of fancy effect yarns or metallic type. Fig 2.7 shows examples of fancy yarns.

Fig 2.7　Fancy Yarns

The fancy yarns are usually made by the irregular plying of staple or continuous filament yarns, and they are characterized by abrupt, periodic effects. The periodicity of this effect is may be random or uniform. These fancy effects are more often generated by the programmed twist variation or by the change of feeding rate of one or more components during plying.

Metallic novelty yarns are characterized by a glittering appearance and a rectangular cross-sectional shape. Durability is added to the metallic yarns by protecting with a transparent film like the aluminum foil or metallized material that produces the glittering effect. Acetate and maylar metallic yarns are examples of this categories.

Section Three　Fabric
第三节　织物(面料)

目前,纺织面料的种类很多,按加工工艺不同,纺织面料可分为机织物、针织物、编织物和非织造布,面料的成分、结构、平方米质量(克重)、后处理等直接影响服装的性能,纺织贸易人员必须掌握基本的面料知识,才能有效地在相应的行业开展业务。

1.Overview of Textile Fabric 面料概述

Non-woven fabric is that fabric produced directly from webs or fibers by bonding, fusing or interlocking. But manufacturing of fabric from yarns is the most common method for a wide range of versatile use. See Fig 2.8 examples of textile fabrics.

Fig 2.8　Textile Fabrics

Yarns or filaments are further processed to produce clothes (fabric) or other textile products, generally by processes such as weaving, knitting, braiding, crocheting . Fabrics are not only used for apparel purpose but also used for curtains, bed linens, industrial applications, etc.

Woven fabrics manufactured by interlacement of two sets of yarns in definite order. Whereas knitted fabrics manufactured by inter-meshing or interlooping of loops of yarn. Braided fabrics are similar to woven fabrics formed by three or more sets.

Non-woven fabrics are manufactured by bonding of fibers by means of chemical, mechanical, thermal(heat), or by solvent treatment. The felting and fusing are the types of non-woven production.

Fabric can be defined as any planar substance constructed from solutions, fibers, yarns in combination. But textile fabric can be defined as slightly different way.Basically, there are the main mechanical methods to manufacture fabric from yarn, such as interweaving, interlooping, intertwining and twisting.

2.Woven Fabric 机织物

Interweaving is the process in which there is intersection or interlace of two sets of straight threads to make woven fabric. Here one set of yarn is called warp yarn which lays in lengthwise of fabric and another set of yarn is called weft yarn which lays as picks or filling in crosswise of fabric.

It is the most common method of fabric production. This process has been used from the ancient period to produce fabric. In interweavingprocess, we can get straight-edge fabric continuous length contained. Fig 2.9 shows the structure of the simplest type of interweaving.

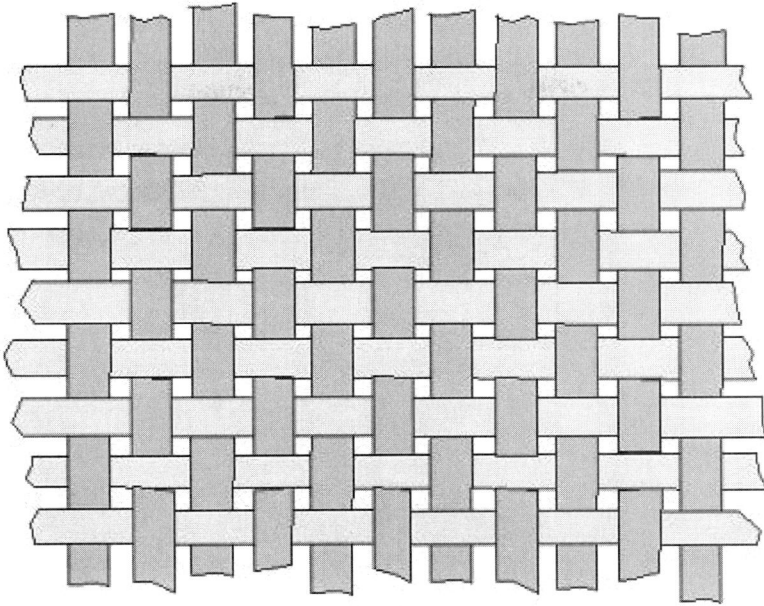

Fig 2.9　The Structure of the Simplest Type of Interweaving

3.Knitted Fabric 针织物

Interlooping consists of forming yarn into loops, each of which is typically only released after a succeeding loop has been formed. There has been intermeshed with the loop so that a secure ground loop structure is achieved. The loops are also held together by the yarn passing from one to the next. Knitting is the most common method of interlooping, and is the second mostly used ways of producing fabric from yarn. Fig 2.10 shows interloping.

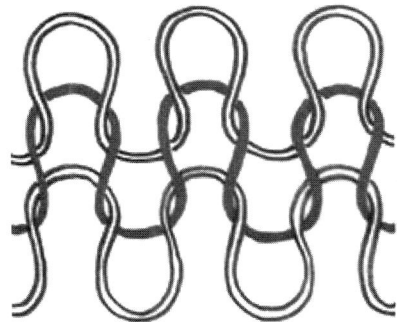

Fig 2.10　Interlooping

4.Braided Fabric 编织物

There are various types of techniques of intertwining and twisting (Fig 2.11) such as braiding, knotting. In intertwining the yarn or threads are caused to intertwine in right angle or in any other angles. These techniques tend to produce special construction which is limited for special purpose.

5.Non-woven Fabric 非织造布

Another method is to manipulate fiber directly into textile fabrics which is so called non-woven process. It is a new branch of textile industry. But this branch is expanding in great number forits high production rates with lower cost (Fig 2.12).

Fig 2.11   Intertwining and Twisting

Fig 2.12   Non-woven

So, here it is clear that there are four types of fabrics: woven fabric (by interweaving method), and knitted fabric (by interlooping method), and braided fabric (by intertwining/twisting method), and non-woven fabric (by non-woven process).

Section Four   Manufacturing of Textiles
第四节   纺织品生产流程

从纤维到纺织品,中间要经过十几道连续过程。产品不同所使用的设备不同,加工工艺也不同。作为纺织贸易业务员,必须掌握基本的纺织品生产流程,了解不同纺织品所使用的基本设备类型,本节介绍典型的纺织品生产流程。

Here, introduce to you the production steps, from fiber to finished garment. See Fig 2.13.

1.Fiber Production 纤维生产

All textiles are made up of fibers that are arranged in different ways to create the desired strength, durability, appearance and texture. The fibers can be of countless origins, but can be grouped into four main categories. Natural fibers, with the exception of silk, have a relatively short fi-

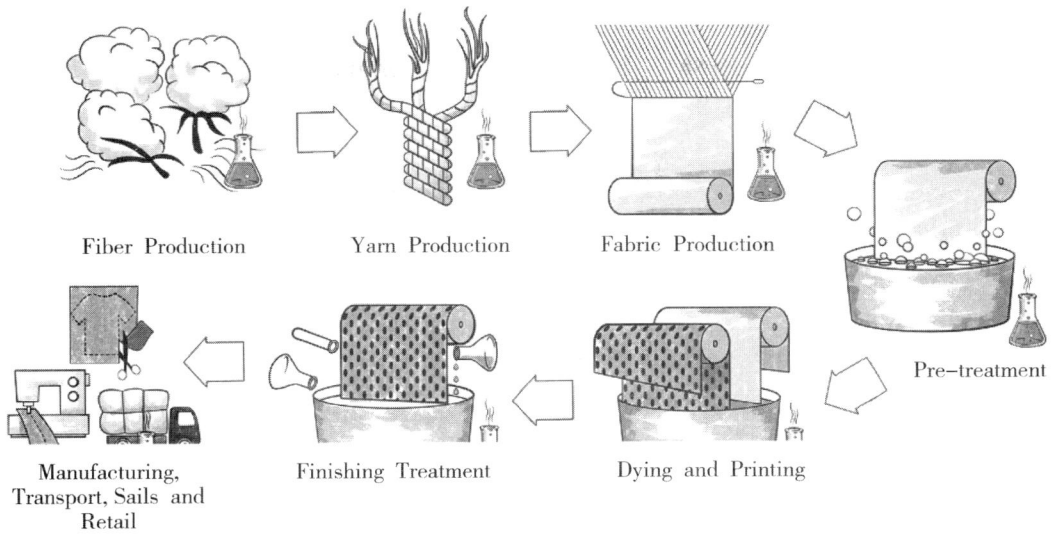

Fiber Production   Yarn Production   Fabric Production

Pre-treatment

Manufacturing,   Finishing Treatment   Dying and Printing
Transport, Sails and
Retail

Fig 2.13   The Textile Processes

ber length, measured in centimetres. Silk and chemical fibers have very long fiber lengths (filaments) ranging from hundreds of metres to kilometres long.

Plant fibers consists of cellulosic material, normally derived from cotton, linen, hemp or bamboo, but more or less any plant with extractable cellulose can be used. Cotton is by far the most commonly used plant fiber and the cultivation of cotton is enormously resource-intensive, with high inputs of water, pesticides, insecticides and fertilisers leaving a large toxic footprint where grown, if not cultivated organically or under specific sustainable conditions. See Fig 2.14.

Fig 2.14   Cotton Harvest

Animal fibers consist of proteins. Wool and silk are the most commonly used fibers from this group, but the wool can come from a number of different animals. In order to make animals grow faster and produce higher yields of wool, pesticides and insecticides are used to prevent disease. Dipping is a common practice to control parasites in sheep farming, making use of both organic phosphates as well as synthetic pyrethroid. After the wool fibers have been sheared they are treated with chemicals during the scouring and washing process.

Chemical fibers such as viscose (rayon) or lyocell are based on cellulosic raw material, normally from wood pulp. They are heavily treated with chemicals before the new fiber is spun. The whole process of producing fibers from wood pulp is very resource-intensive, involving the use of several hazardous substances.

Synthetic fibers are made from monomers sourced from fossil oil feedstocks, which are subsequently polymerised into different fibers. Given all the possible monomers that can be made from a synthetic feedstock, the possible combinations are endless. However the most common synthetic fiber is polyester, followed by polyamide, polyacrylic and aramide. Depending on the monomer used to produce the fiber, an endless number of chemicals may be used in the process. For some of the synthetic fibers such as polyester, dyeing can be accomplished already when the fiber is manufactured.

2.Yarn Production 纱线生产

When the fiber has been harvested or produced the next step is to spin the fibers into a yarn. It is easy to believe that this step, which is a mechanical one, uses no chemicals. But in order to increase the strength of the fiber, increase fiber cohesion and reduce friction during the spinning process, spinning oils are added(Fig 2.15).

Fig 2.15   Ring Spinning

3.Fabric Production 织物生产

The core of textile manufacture is fabric production. Fabrics can be made in many different ways, the most common being weaving, knitting or through production of non-woven fabrics. To prevent the yarn from breaking during these processes, it is important to strengthen the yarn and reduce friction. Sizing chemicals and lubricants are therefore added. See Fig 2.16.

Fig 2.16   Weaving on Air-jet Loom

4.Pre-treatment 预处理

Pre-treatment processes can be carried out with fibers, yarns or fabrics.Subsequent processing of the material needs to be prepared to accept dyes and functional chemicals. This is done in a multi-step process. Exactly which steps the fabric goes through depends on the type, or blend of fiber, and how the fabric will be treated afterwards. In some cases pre-treated fabrics are manufactured for later garment dyeing.

The most common steps involving chemicals for a fabric are as followings.

Washing is the general cleaning of the fabric following previous steps and treatments.

De-sizing removes the sizing chemicals from the warp yarns in the woven fabric.

Scouring removes fatty waxes and greases from natural fibers, cotton seed and husk.

Bleaching makes the fibers whiter and facilitates the dyeing process. It also makes the fibers more absorbent.

Mercerizing makes cellulosic fibers swell and stronger, more lustrous and a greater capacity to accept dye. By doing so one can reduce the amount of dyes needed.

Carbonizing removes vegetable residues such as seed pods from the wool.

5.Dyeing and Printing 染色与印花

During dyeing and printing both hazardous chemicals and dyestuffs are used. Dyes used for dyeing, can also be used for printing, but must then undergo the same fixation and washing steps after the dyeing process. The most common way to print a fabric in full width is to use pigment prints, where the pigments stick to a surface using polymeric resin or a binder. No washing processes are needed. For garmentprinting, plastisol printing is very common. The PVC-based paste often contains hazardous chemicals, such as phthalates, but there are also alternatives based on acrylate or polyurethane.

Dyeing can take place in several steps when processing the textile. It can be done when spinning the synthetic or man-made fibers, as loose natural or regenerated fibers and in the form of yarns or fabrics. Garment dyeing is also common. For fiber blends, two types of dyed fibers can be spunned together e.g. viscose and wool.

Full-width printing is carried out on pre-treated fabrics, but it is also possible to put a print on a garment or manufactured textile product by screen or transfer printing. Digital printing is another method.

There are other printing techniques as discharge and resist print using dyes and chemicals. They involve washing to get rid of surplus dyes and residues.

6.Finishing Treatments 后整理

This step of the process is all about adding special technical properties or an aesthetic appeal to the finished fabric. Depending on the properties desired, such as flame retardance, enhanced water resistance, antibacterial treatment, protective coatings or specific fashion treatments, a diverse range of chemicals are used. Some examples are given below.

Handle modification include several treatments as follows: crease resistance (anti-wrinkling, easy care), antistatic treatment, anti-pilling, antibacterial/anti-odor treatment, water repellance, oil/soil repellance, flame retardance, flame retardants (halogenated, phosphor based), (protective) coatings, laminated films and membranes, garment treatments for fashion.

7.Manufacturing, Transport, Sales and Retail 生产、运输、销售与零售

When the fabric has the desired colour and properties, it is made into finished products such as sweaters, jeans, shoes or other special items like carpets, furniture or car seats. This step includes processes such as cutting, sewing and the addition of buttons and zippers, for example. In some cases dyeing and printing of the finished garments, with the fabric only pre-treated, occur at this step. In garment dyeing there are a lot of dyestuffs and chemicals used (showed in step 5). Some times dyestuffs with quite bad wash permanence are chosen to give the clothing in fashion a worn out look. For garment printing, plastisol prints (PVC) are very common, but there are other types available for example based on acrylate or polyurethane.

Quiz   课后思考题

1. 请用图表的形式阐述纺织纤维的分类。
2. 根据课文,典型的纺织品生产工艺包含哪七个步骤?
3. 纺织品手感处理有哪些方式?
4. 试比较机织工艺和针织工艺的区别。
5. 短纤维纱线的四大生产系统是什么?

Chapter Three   Enter into a Contract
第三章   签订合同

　　建立业务关系是开展纺织出口贸易的基础。纺织出口商应通过各种商务网站和展会等形式向国外客商直接宣传,增进公司产品在国际市场的知名度,对重点贸易对象发送希望建立贸易业务的信函,与其建立贸易伙伴关系,从而拓展本公司的业务规模。出口交易磋商有口头和书面形式。在业务初期,一般通过电子邮件或传真进行洽谈,买卖双方主要就品名、品质、数量、包装、价格、装运、支付、保险、商品检验、不可抗力、索赔和仲裁等合同条款进行洽谈并取得一致意见,最终签订合同。本章将通过具体案例介绍业务关系的建业、交易条款的磋商和合同签订的整个过程。

Section One   Establishment of Business Relationship
第一节   建立业务关系

　　江苏 RQ 纺织品有限公司是一家当地的外贸公司,公司通过 Alibaba 等平台向海外买家展示产品,进而获得贸易商机和订单。王杰是公司的外贸业务员,通过 Google 搜索到了美国森泰纺织公司的电子邮箱,用电子邮件向该公司发出建立贸易业务关系函,希望和该公司建立业务关系。

1.Company Profile 公司简介

Jiangsu RQ Textile Co., Ltd has been well established since 2005 in Jiangsu, China. It is especially experienced in manufacturing complicated knitwear. They gear their market position toward high quality at a reasonable price for the buyers. For the last three decades, RQ has developed from a small family business into a company of considerable size. At the moment, they employed around 1,000 staffs.

It has produced various kinds of woven fabrics for lady's wear, men's wear, and children's wear. Moreover, they also use different kinds of materials, such as polyester, cotton, linen, acrylic. They have sophisticated experiences in manufacturing high quality knitted garment.

In order to achieve continuous improvements, RQ actively participates in different kinds of exhibitions, develops e-commerce on the internet, and aims to continue providing best services and the highest quality products to the customers around the world.

2.Business Letter 商务信函

　　江苏 RQ 纺织品有限公司于 2017 年 9 月 9 日通过互联网的方式给美国森泰纺织公司发了一封电子邮件,简单介绍了自己的公司,并表达了与对方建立业务关系的期望。以下是邮件的内容。

From：Jiangsu RQ Textile Co., Ltd
779 East Dongfeng Road, Yancheng, Jiangsu, China
Tel：+86-515-12345678　Fax：2345678
E-mail：glip@ 163.com

To：United States SenTai Textile Trade Co., LTD
23North Street, New York, The United States
Tel：+1-781-7698550　Fax：+1-781-7699468
E-mail：btcl@ hotmail.com

Date：September 9th, 2017

Dear Sir or Madam,

We are pleased to obtain your name from thewebsite. We know that your company is of good standing and reliability in New York. We understand that you are particularly interested in the import of 100% cotton yarn-dyed fabric from China.

In recent years, we have done business with the largest and most prominentcompanies in your area. We are confident that we will be able to offer you the satisfied fabrics if the delivery, price and quality meet our requirements.

We look forward to establishing good business relationship with you soon.

Yours sincerely,
Jie Wang
Manager of Export Department

Section Two　　Business Negotiation
第二节　业务磋商

　　国际贸易磋商的基本流程包括询盘、发盘、还盘和接受四个环节,这一经典交易流程在很长时间里规范着各国商人的行为,使得交易顺利开展。虽然随着互联网的发展,该流程发生了很大变化,交易方式也变得更加简单化、直接化和弹性化,但这一流程的影响还存在,熟悉这些环节仍有很大的借鉴意义。本节通过江苏 RQ 纺织品有限公司和美国森泰纺织贸易有限公司业务磋商的具体事例,对业务磋商流程进行介绍。

1.Inquiry 询盘

　　(1)定义。询盘又叫询价,是准备购买或出售商品的人向潜在的供货人或买主询问该商品的成交条件或交易的可能性的业务行为。询盘可以由买方发出,也可以由卖方发出。

　　(2)目的。是了解对方的需求(产品)及成交条件。询盘不是实盘,对询盘人不具有约束力。询盘对象应该广泛一些。在写询问信时要注意以下问题:要简明、准确、清楚地陈述自己的要求;不要提及自己掌握的限价,以防止被客户摸到底线;确保询问简洁、有礼,切忌拖沓。

下面是来自美国森泰纺织贸易有限公司的保罗先生于2017年9月12日江苏RQ纺织品有限公司王杰先生发出的一项询盘。

From：United States SenTai Textile Trade Co.，LTD
23North Street，New York，The United States
Tel：+1-781-7698550　Fax：+1-781-7699468
E-mail：btcl@ hotmail.com

To：Jiangsu RQ Textile Co.，Ltd
779 East Dongfeng Road,Yancheng，Jiangsu，China
Tel：+86-515-12345678　Fax：2345678
E-mail：glip@ 163.com

Date：September 12th，2017

Dear Sir，
From the letter we have received on Sept. 9，we find that you are an exporter of the 100% cotton yarn-dyed fabrics. At present，we are interested in your goods fine in quality and low in price. It would be highly appreciated if you could send us details and samples for our reference and quote your lowest price on CIF New York basis including our 3% commission.

We are looking forward to your early reply.

Yours sincerely，
Paul Jonson

询盘要点见表3-1。

表3-1　美国森泰纺织贸易有限公司询盘要点

进口商	美国森泰纺织品贸易有限公司
出口商	江苏RQ纺织品有限公司
日期	2017年9月12日
品名	全棉色织物
贸易方式	CIF纽约
佣金	3%
其他	附寄产品详细情况及报价

2.Offer 发盘

(1)定义。发盘又叫报价,是买方或卖方向对方提出各项交易条件,并愿意按照这些条件达成交易,是订立合同的一种确定的表示。发盘必须是确定的,如果在以上的信件最后标明

"仅供参考"等不确定字样,则构不成发盘,只是和买方商讨而已。

(2)构成要件。根据《联合国国际货物销售合同公约》规定,发盘应包括以下三个方面的内容:要准确标明货物的名称、规格;应明示或默示规定货物的数量或规定确定数量的方法;应明示或默示规定货物的价格或规定确定价格的方法。

凡包括以上三要素的要约,即可构成发盘,发盘如果被接受,合同即告成立。

对于客户的询盘,江苏 RQ 纺织品有限公司迅速做出反应,下面是 2017 年 9 月 14 日对美国森泰纺织贸易有限公司的保罗先生发出的发盘。

From：Jiangsu RQ Textile Co.，Ltd

779 East Dongfeng Road，Yancheng，Jiangsu，China

Tel：+86-515-12345678　Fax：2345678

E-mail：glip@ 163.com

To：United States SenTai Textile Trade Co.，LTD

23North Street，New York，The United States

Tel：+1-781-7698550　Fax：+1-781-7699468

E-mail：btcl@ hotmail.com

Date：September 14th，2017

Dear Paul Johnson，

In reply to your inquiry of September 12th，2017 asking us to make an offer for our 100% cotton yarn-dayed fabric，we are pleased to make you a quotation along with related conditions as follows.

Article：100% cotton yarn-dyed fabric

Design：No. JH486

Specification：58" 42×42s 118×78

Weight：100-110g/m^2

Minimum Quantity：1000m/color，5000m/order

Packing：30-40m into a plastic bag，5 plastic bags into a carton

Price：US$ 1.52/m CIFC3% New York

Shipment：30-90 days after receiving your L/C or T/T deposit depending on your order size，from Shanghai to New York

Payment：By confirmed irrevocable L/C payable by draft at sight or T/T

We hope the above terms and conditions will be acceptable to you and await with keen interest your first order.

Yours faithfully，

Wang Jie

发盘要点见表 3-2。

表 3-2　江苏 RQ 纺织品有限公司发盘要点

客户	美国森泰纺织贸易有限公司
日期	2017 年 9 月 14 日
品名	全棉色织物面料
式样	JH486 号
规格	58"　42×42s　118×78
克重量	100~110g/m^2
最小起订量	1000 米/色,5000 米/订单
包装	打卷包装,30~40 米装入一个塑料袋,5 个塑料袋装入一个纸箱
价格	每米 1.52 美元 CIF 价到纽约,含 3% 的佣金
装运	在收到信用证或 T/T 后 1~3 个月之后装运,从上海港到纽约港
付款	T/T 或不可撤销的信用证以即期汇票支付

3.Counter-offer 还盘

还盘又叫还价,是指受盘人不同意或不完全同意发盘人在发盘中提起的条件,为了进一步协商,对发盘提出修改或变更的意见。还盘实际上是对原发盘的拒绝,同时,也是受盘人向原发盘人做出的一项新的发盘。还盘一旦做出,原发盘即失去效力,同时,还盘一方与原发盘人在地位上发生变换,分别成为新的发盘人和受盘人。因而,与发盘一样,还盘也存在一个效力问题,这与发盘一致,只有具有约束力的还盘才能成为一项新的发盘。

保罗先生仔细考虑之后,于 2017 年 9 月 17 日还盘如下。

From：United States SenTai Textile Trade Co.，LTD
23North Street，New York，The United States
Tel：+1-781-7698550　Fax：+1-781-7699468
E-mail：btcl@ hotmail.com

To：Jiangsu RQ Textile Co.，Ltd
779 East Dongfeng Road,Yancheng，Jiangsu，China
Tel：+86-515-12345678　Fax：2345678
E-mail：glip@ 163.com

Date：September 17th，2017

Dear Mr. Wang,
We acknowledge with thanks the receipt of your letter of September 14th，2017 for 100% cotton yarn-dyed fabrics at $1.52 per meter CIFC3% New York.

We regret to tell you that your price has been found too high to be acceptable. Under such circumstance, you would leave us with no room for profit. If you can make a reduction in your price, say to $1.38, there is a possibility of getting this business done. And we will order 20,000 meters of fabric for No. JH486 in 5 colors with you.

Waiting for your early reply.

Sincerely yours,
Paul Johnson

还盘要点见表3-3。

表3-3   美国森泰纺织品贸易有限公司还盘要点

品名	全棉色织物
规格	JH486 号
价格	CIFC3% 到纽约 1.38 美元/米
数量	20000m
颜色	5 色

4.Acceptance 接受

接受指买方或卖方同意对方在发盘中提出的各项交易条件,并愿意按这些条件达成交易,订立合同的一种确定的表示。是双方订立合同的必要环节。表示接受有两种方式:一是声明,可以是口头声明也可以以书面形式表示;二是做出行为,通常指由卖方发出货物或由买方支付货款。

王杰经过与公司协商,决定接受对方的还盘,下面是 2017 年 9 月 20 日王杰先生向保罗先生发出的一封接受邮件。

From：Jiangsu RQ Textile Co.，Ltd
779 East Dongfeng Road,Yancheng, Jiangsu, China
Tel：+86-515-12345678   Fax：2345678
E-mail：glip@ 163.com

To：United States SenTai Textile Trade Co.，LTD
23North Street, New York, The United States
Tel：+1-781-7698550   Fax：+1-781-7699468
E-mail：btcl@ hotmail.com

Date：September 20th, 2017

Dear Mr. Paul,

We thank you for your letter giving us a counter-offer for20,00 meters of 100% cotton yarn-dyed fabric.

Although your price is close to our rock bottom, we have finally decided to accept your counter-offer of USD 1.38 per meter CIF New York with a view of initiating our business with you at an early date. And other terms and conditions are unchanged.

Sincerely yours,

Wang Jie

接受要点如下:我方接受贵方的还盘,以每米 1.38 美元的价格成交,其他条款和条件不变。

至此,交易磋商阶段的四个环节——询盘、发盘、还盘、接受全部结束,买卖双方就交易各项条款达成一致,交易有了实质性进展。接下来,按照买方的要求,江苏 RQ 公司完成打样并及时将样品寄出。

Section Three　　Contract
第三节　合同

在纺织品国际贸易中,合同主要采用两种形式:一种是条款完备、内容较全面的正式合同,如销售合同(sales contract);另一种是内容较简单的简式合同,如销售确认书(sales confirmation)。两者虽然在格式、条款项目和内容的繁简上有所不同,但在法律上具有同等效力,对买卖双方均有约束力,本节将通过江苏 RQ 纺织品有限公司和美国森泰纺织贸易有限公司签订的销售合同为例进行介绍。

A contract is an agreement between two or more competent parties in which an offer is made and accepted, and each party benefits. It is an agreement which sets forth binding obligations of the relevant parties. The agreement can be formal, informal, written, oral or just plain understood. Some contracts are required to be in writing in order to be enforced. This term, in its more extensive sense, includes every description of agreement, or obligation, whereby one party becomes bound to another to pay a sum of money, or to do or omit to do a certain act. In its more confined sense, it is an agreement between two or more persons, concerning something to be done, whereby both parties are bound to each other, or one is bound to the other.

A contract properly includes: ①the full name and address of the buyer and the seller; ②the commodities involved; ③all the terms and conditions agreed upon; ④indication of the number of original copies of the contract, the language used, the term of validity and possible extension of the contract. In international trade, export and import contracts vary in both names and forms. The names that often appear are contract, confirmation, agreement and memorandum.

美国森泰纺织贸易有限公司于 2017 年 9 月 29 日收到江苏 RQ 纺织品有限公司样品后确认其品质,双方按事先约定的条款订立以下合同。

SALES CONTRACT

The Buyer: United States SenTai Textile Trade Co., LTD Date: October 2, 2017

The Seller: Jiangsu RQ Textile Co., Ltd   No.: JX760125

The contract is made by and between the seller and the buyer, whereby the seller agrees to sell and the buyer agrees to buy the under-mentioned goods according to the terms and conditions stipulated below:

Article No.	Name of Commodity	Specification	Color	Quantity (Meter)	Unit Price (USD/M, CIF New York C3)	Amount
JH486-1			black	5,000	1.38	6,900.00
JH486-2		Width:58" Yarn count:	gray	5,000	1.38	6,900.00
JH486-3	100% cotton yarn-dyed	42s×42s	off-white	5,000	1.38	6,900.00
JH486-4		Weight:100- 110g/m²	orang	3,000	1.38	4,140.00
JH486-5			chocolate	2,000	1.38	2,760.00
Total				20,000		27,600.00

Say US dollars twenty-seven thousand six hundred only.

Terms and Conditions:

5% more or less both in amount and quantity is allowed.

Packing: 30-40m into a plastic bag, 5 plastic bags into a carton.

Port of Loading: Shanghai, China.

Port of Destination: New York, USA.

Shipping Mark: N/M.

Date of shipment: Not later than December 20, 2017 By Vessel.

Terms of payment: By confirmed irrevocable L/C payable by draft at sight.

Partial Shipment: Prohibited.

Transshipment: Prohibited.

Insurance: To be effected by the sellers for 110% of full invoice value.

Documents required:

        Manually signed Commercial Invoice in quadruplicate;

        Full set of clean on board oceanBills of Lading made out to our order;

        Signed Packing List in quadruplicate;

        Signed Certificate of Origin in duplicate;

        Insurance Policy in duplicate;

        Beneficiary's Certificate.

The Seller:Jiangsu RQ Textile Co., Ltd   The Buyer: United States SenTai Textile Trade Co., LTD

        Wang Jie   Paul Johnson

Quiz   课后思考题

1. 外贸磋商过程一般包括哪些步骤？其中哪些是必要的？

2. 请说明课文中外贸合同各条款的内容。

3. 发给外商客户的,介绍自己公司的"开发信"应该包含哪些内容。

4. 在交易磋商的过程中,买家一般都不希望卖家报价过高而要求降价,作为卖家,可以从哪些角度试图说明价格的合理性,并说服对方接受?

Chapter Four　Smaple Management
第四章　样品跟单

　　样品通常是从一批商品中抽出来的或由生产、使用部门设计、加工出来的,足以反映和代表整批商品品质的少量实物。在国际贸易中,凡以样品表示商品品质并以此作为交货依据的,称为"凭样买卖"。如为卖方提供样品,须在买方确认后对该样品注明标号;如由买方提供样品,卖方应依样加工复制,交由买方确认;凡经买方确认的样品称为"确认样品"(approval sample),一旦其被纳入合同条款,便成为"成交样",是日后买卖双方交货与验货的实物依据。本章将分别从买卖双方角度,认识外贸跟单中与样品相关的知识。

Section One　How to Request a Sample
第一节　索要样品

　　本节从美国买家的角度,以阿里巴巴电商平台为例,讲述了向中国供应商索要样品的要点和技巧。由于外国客商样品跟单的惯常做法与国内存在差异,这会带来一些沟通上的困难,从这些差距中可以了解买方对于样品的关注点,跟单员才能更好地配合客户顺利收到所需的样品。

　　Once you've settled on a supplier, it's time to procure a sample product. When importing from Alibaba, a major concern is product quality and a practical way to control this is to request a product sample from your supplier in China.

1.Specifying Details When Asking for a Sample 索要样品时应列明细节

　　Communication styles differ in China and the US. Because of these cultural differences, it's necessary to be specific when requesting a sample from your supplier.

　　Details specified on the phone or by email are not always adhered to by the supplier. The reasons for this is that the chain of command in factories is not always direct and there may be two or more people the message delivers before it gets to the person who's actually making the sample. In between, information can get confused or lost so, as you may expect, the person creating the sample may receive different instructions than what you relayed.

　　After each email or telephone chat, you should follow up with written details about how you want the sample produced. You should include the following bullet points.

　　a. The address you want the sample sent to, with a specification that the sample be labeled "sample: of no commercial value." This will save you from being charged duty for the package.

　　b. Specifics about the product that contain as much detail as possible. You could even include a diagram. No detail is too small: for example, one small business ordered a sample of a plush snowman toy and it came with carrot eyes. Be aware that what you think of as obvious, may not be. Take the time to be specific.

c. Many of the manufacturers on Alibaba will agree to test the product before sending it to you, so feel free to ask.

d. Ask your supplier in China to include a model number and company name tag so you don't get their samples confused with other samples you may be ordering.

e. An indication that the sample needs to be a working sample as it will undergo tests once it arrives. (While you may be planning minimal testing, specifying that you need a working sample will help insure you're getting a high-quality sample.)

f. Some other tips on clear communication with your supplier in China.

g. Every reputable manufacturer on Alibaba will be used to working with clear deadlines and should be able to communicate a timeframe for samples. Make sure you ask for their process and timeframe, that way you'll know when you can ask for changes and when it should be on its way to you.

h. Include diagrams and drawings of what you expect the sample to look like.

i. If you're worried that there may be confusion, ask your supplier to confirm the specs they're using to create your sample. You should be able to tell quite quickly if they've understood what you're asking for.

j. Ask to do a video chat with your supplier once the sample is completed so you can see what it looks like before it is shipped. Perhaps modifications can be made before shipping which would save both you and your supplier in China money.

2.Notifications Before You Sign off on the Pre-production Sample from China 在确认产前样之前的注意事项

Ask how the product will differ from the sample in mass production. Sometimes the same material is not available in small quantities for a sample. Many of the manufacturers in China produce tens of thousands of each product, so a one-off sample will most likely have at least a few differences. Sometimes the sample is handmade by the supplier, or made on a different machine than will be used for mass production.

Remember that the invoice is very important in China, and that any details or variations from the sample you expect the product to have should be specified there.

3.Paying for Your Sample 支付样品费

There is usually no way around paying for your sample product from Alibaba. However, here are a few tips that may help reduce the cost of ordering a sample or even getting one for free.

Some other tips on clear communication with your supplier in China.

a. Explain that if the sample meets your requirements you will place a large order. Many manufacturers on Alibaba will agree to subtract the sample costs out of your first order.

b. State that you expect to do business exclusively with this supplier in China.

c. Ask your supplier from Alibaba to add the sample cost to your official order. This way if you decide to order from another supplier you will save the sample cost.

d. Offer to split the costs with your supplier in China.

e. Once you've settled on a price for the sample from Alibaba, the easiest, fastest, and completely secure way to make a wire transfer to China is using Veem. Your supplier in China will thank you for making payment quickly and safely.

Section Two　　E-mail Communication on Samples
第二节　　邮件沟通样品细节

在国际贸易中,如样品为国外客户提供,在收到客户发来的电子邮件和样品后,应及时联系相关的生产部门,依样加工复制,并掌握样品生产情况。此外,要及时写邮件告知客户关于复制样的具体意见和价格,同时告知回样何时做好并寄去,有时候,一件样品的确认过程,需要十几封甚至更多电子邮件沟通解决。

1.Receipt of Samples 收到样品

收件人	ralph2566@ hotmail. com
主题	Samples

Hi.Ralph,

How are youdoing?

We are pleased to confirm the receipt of your comforter cover samples of Art. No. 2356 and 2357. After discussing with the technicians of our factory, we can assure you that we could make the goods you required entirely satisfactory to you.

The price of Art. No 2356 should be USD13.20/set and Art. No 2357 is USD15.70/set. All the prices are on CIF Long Beach basis. Our factory is ready to make the duplicate samples for your confirmation. If the samples are satisfactory to you and the prices are acceptable, we hope we could receive your trial order soon.

For your information, we will send the duplicate samples to you by FedEx within one week.

Best regards,

Linda Xu

要点解读:卖方告知买方已收到对方寄来的样品,并保证可以生产出对方满意的产品,同时对两款产品进行报价,最后向对方承诺可以在一周内寄出复制样。

2.Alternative Material 替代材料

收件人   Linda2009@ hotmail. com

主题   Re：Samples

Dear Linda,

How are things going on with you?

We received your samples yesterday with many thanks.

After checking with our manufacturer, we find your price is obviously out of line with the prevailing market because the price forcotton has risen dramatically since last year. In this case, your price will leave us no profit. So I strongly recommend T/C 65/35 as an ideal substitute for cotton.

We will send you our samples fabrics made of T/C 65/35 soon, once you've recived them, please let us know if you produce those two items on the new material and meet our target prices. and hope you accept our plan.

Looking forward to yoursoonest reply.

Best regards,

Ralph

要点解读:原材料上涨导致报价过高,买家难以承受的情况非常常见,在该邮件中,买方提出使用成本相对较低的涤棉混纺织物作为原料,替代棉织物。

3.Sample Making and Shipping 打样与寄样

收件人   ralph2566@ hotmail. com

主题   Re：Re：Samples

Dear Ralph,

I have received the fabric samples you sent. Thank you very much and we think you've made a very constructive proposal. And the prices you quoted seem acceptable to us, too.

We'll start making the new samples based on T/C 65/35 material this week. Hopefully, you'll get our samples next week. I think there's a good chance we'll get this business done.

Regarding the sample making and shipping fees, as a usual practice, we require our potential customers to pay for the fees, but we'll pay you back when you place the first order with us. Hope you kindly understand.

Thank you and keep in touch.

Best wishes,
Linda Xu

要点解读:在纺织和其他行业,使用现成的材料和规格制作样品一般成本较低,但改用新材料或新规格往往会产生较多的"打样费",对于潜在的客户,往往采用"先由对方支付,待对方下单后给予退还"的做法,这样可以避免买方只索要样品而不下订单的被动局面。

Quiz   课后思考题

1. 请简述样品在国际贸易中的重要性？
2. 外贸跟单中,按功能分,样品有哪些类型？分别起什么作用？
3. 客户打样费用一般是由哪方来承担？
4. 在样品跟单过程中,作为卖方可以通过哪些方式确保样品满足买方要求。

Chapter Five   Quality of Commodity
第五章   质量跟单

在纺织国际贸易中,当和国外客户确定样品后进入大货生产阶段,此时须将外贸合同转化为加工合同,并组织和落实生产。为了控制货物品质,跟单员必须深入加工企业,与加工企业一起制订严格的生产品质控制计划,按工艺要求进行有效控制,对成品进行查验并编写检验报告,如发现品质异常,应与加工企业一起查找原因,及时采取有效措施。

Section One   Introduction to Quality
第一节   质量概述

要做好产品质量跟单,跟单员首先要了解和掌握产品质量要素构成,在跟单过程中,针对产品质量要素,参考国家产品质量标准、客商要求,监督产品生产的全过程,及时解决产品生产过程中出现的问题。通过本节学习,学生应掌握纺织产品质量要素的互构成。

Quality of goods is indispensable to international trade. Whether it is visible trade or invisible trade, and the quality of a certain kind of goods determines, to a great degree, its market and price. Therefore, the quality of the goods is among the main terms upon which a sales contract is based and constructed.

Commodity provides the material basis for international trade. All commodities presentcertain qualities. Therefore, the quality of commodity is not only one of the major terms of sales contract, but also the first item which should be agreed upon by the exporter and the importer while the business is being negotiated. The seller must deliver the goods that are of quality required by the contract, the failure of which will result in the disputes between the seller and the buyer. Thus, due consideration should be given to the matters of quality of the commodity transacted. That's to say that the seller must deliver goods that are of the quality required by the contract. If the goods do not conform to the contract, the buyer will be entitled to lodge a claim for damages. Therefore, at the time of the conclusion of the contract, the quality should be clearly stipulated.

In export trade, the superior or inferior quality of a certain commodity has an immediate bearing not only on the use and price of the commodity, but also on the sale and reputation of it. On the one hand, with the intensifying competition in international market, manufacturers in different countries make great efforts to promote the sale of their products by improving the quality of them. The commodity with superior quality always enjoys good market. On the other hand, the importer would only purchase those goods of certain quality in which he is particular interested. Both the seller and the buyer express deep concern at the quality of commodity.

The quality of goods refers to the intrinsic attributes and the outer form or shape of thegoods, such as modeling, structure, color, luster, taste, chemical composition, mechanical performance, biological features, etc. In another sense, a certain kind of goods possesses both natural and social attributes. From a narrow point of view, it possesses natural attributes, while from a broad point of view, it also includes its social attributes, which is how it meets the subjective requirements and different tastes of its customers.

The quality of commodity is the combination of the intrinsic quality and outside formor shape of the commodity, such as modeling, structure, color, luster, chemical composition, mechanical performance, biological features, etc. The qualities of different commodities can be pressed in different ways. The methods of stipulating quality of commodity depend on the quality, character and the customary usage in practice. In international trade, there are two ways to indicate the quality of the goods either by description or by sample.

Section Two Methods of Stipulating Quality of Commodity
第二节 货物品质的表示方法

货物品质是买卖双方关注的要点,按照不同行业不同产品,国际贸易中成交商品(标的物)的品质表示有多种方式,各种方式各有其优缺点,作为跟单员应了解这些表示方法,在跟单业务中及时掌握产品的品质状况。本节介绍两种外贸跟单中常用的货物品质表示方法:凭文字说明和凭样品。

1.Sale by Description 凭文字说明买卖

In the international trade, mostly the goods are sold by the method of sale by specification, grade or standard except some special cases. This method may be further classified into the following types.

(1) Sale by specification, grade or standard

The specification of the goods refers to certain main indicators which indicate the quality of the goods, such as composition, content, purity, size, length, thickness. Sale by specification is a sales way of convenience and accuracy. So in practice it is most widely used. Goods with different quality should have different standards, and for those with different application there are also different standards.

(2) Sale by brand name or trade mark

Brand name or trade mark is based on high quality, which is used by the manufacturers to distinguish theirhigh-quality goods with the others of the like. Brand is the name of the goods, while trade mark is the tag. They are related to each other closely. As to the goods whose quality is stable' reputation is sound and with which the customers are quite familiar, we may sell it by brand name or trade mark. For example, "Maxam Dental Cream" "Haier Air Conditioner" "Toyota Automobile", etc.

Since these goods with the same brand name or trade mark possess the same quality and their quality remain unified and unchanged, their brand names or trademarks are often used to indicate the quality of these goods. Such a method is called "sale by brand name or trade mark".

(3) Sale by name of origin

Some goods, just like some agricultural products and by-products subject to the influence of nature and traditional production techniques, are well known by their origins for their excellent quality all over the world. As to these products, the origins may well indicate their qualities. These goods can be sold by name of origin.

(4) Sale by description and illustration

The quality of some commodities, such as large-sized machines technological instruments, electric machines can not be simply indicated by quality indexes, instead it is quite necessary to explain in detail the structure, material, performance as well as method of operation. Thus, the specific descriptions of products are required to indicate the quality of the goods. If necessary, pictures, photos, etc. must also be provided.

2.Sale by Sample 凭样品买卖

Sale by sample refers to the transaction method which is done by the sample confirmed by both the buyer and the seller.

The sample refers to the article which can be used to represent the quality of the whole lot. In merchandising, a sample is a small quantity of a product, often taken out from a whole lot or specially designed and processed, that is given to encourage prospective customers to buy the product. The transaction that is concluded on the basis of the sample representing the quality ofthe whole lot can be called sales by sample. This method is used when the transaction is hard to conclude by standard, grade or words, such as some certain arts and crafts products, garmenture, local specialty, light industrial products, etc.

Sale by sample includes 3 cases, i.e., sale by the seller's sample, sale by the buyer's sample and sale by the counter sample.

(1)Sale by the seller's sample

Seller's samples are the samples which are usually sent by the seller to the buyer, which is also called original sample.

In this case, the seller shall supply a representative sample which will possess the moderate quality among a large quantity of the physical goods, and at the same time keep a duplicate sample, which shall be inquality as or on the whole as the same as the standard sample.The sample dispatched and the duplicate sample/file sample kept shall have the same article number so as to make it convenient for delivery, verification when handling quality disputes or future transactions.

(2)Sale by the buyer's sample

a. In this case, the seller shall first take into consideration the availability of the new material and the possibility of providing the processing technology.

b.In order to take the initiative, the seller may reproduce the buyer's sample, i. e., counter sample, and send it back to the buyer as a type sample. After the buyer confirms the counter sample sale by the buyer's sample is changed into sale by the seller's counter sample.

c. The two parties shall stipulate that in case the buyer's sample results in any disputes of infringement of industrial property, the seller will have nothing to do with it.

（3）Sale by the counter sample

Samples can be also provided by the buyer. They are given as the quality standard for the products to be produced and delivered by the seller. Under such circumstances, to avoid future disputesover the quality of the goods, the seller usually first duplicates the samples and then sends the duplicate to the buyer for confirmation. This sample is called counter sample.

3.Additional Tips on Sample 样品品质补充信息

In international trade practice, if sale by samplesadopted, the followings should be paid attention to.

a. We should try to do the business by "sale by the seller's sample".

b. When the seller sends out the sample, it is better that the seller will keep the "original" or "duplicate"sample so as to make it convenient for verification when handling quality disputes or future transactions.

c. If the transaction is done by "sale by the buyer's sample", we should pay attention to the fact that whether the sample of the buyer has something to do with the problems of politics, society and religion, such as color, pattern and design. We should also take into consideration the availability of the new material and the possibility of providing the processing technology in order to avoid the unnecessary trouble in delivery. For the sake of caution, the import and export enterprises usually make it clear as in the remarks in the contract that "For any cotton price goods produced with the designs, trade marks, brands and/or stampings provided by the buyers, should there be any dispute arising from infringement upon the third party's industrial property right, it is the buyer to be held responsible for it".

d. When we get the sample of the buyer, it is better to make it as counter sample.

e. Whether it is sale by buyer's sample or by sellers' sample, if it is difficult to keep the goods contracted in strict accordance with the sample, the seller should write some flexible terms in the sales contract as follows: shipment shall be similar to the sample, quality to be about equal to the sample, quality to be nearly same as the sample.

f. Whether it is sale by buyer's sample or by seller's sample, if it is necessary, sometimes "sealed sample" can be adopted.

Section Three   Quality Latitude and Quality Tolerance
第三节   品质机动幅度条款和品质公差条款

由于纺织品本身的特性,如漂白布的幅宽,在加工过程中一般规定为某一范围均为合格,所以,在外贸中允许卖方所交货物的品质指标在一定幅度内有所灵活,这一规定称为品质机动幅度。此外,对于纱线支数等指标,由于在生产过程中不能做到非常精确,可根据国际惯例或经买卖双方协商同意,对合同中的品质指标订有允许的"公差",这一规定称为品质公差。作为纺织从业人员,必须了解品质机动幅度条款和品质公差条款。

1. Overview of Quality Latitude and Tolerance 品质机动幅度和品质公差概述

In international trade, the seller should strictly abide by the terms specified in thecontract. The quality delivered by the seller should be in strict conformity with the terms and conditions in the contract. But for some goods there will be natural consumption during productions, and the affection of production process, the goods own characteristics, it is very hard to deliver the goods as per the terms and conditions stated in the contract. For such goods, if the stipulations are too firm or quality criterions too fixed, it bring the seller a lot of trouble in delivery. Consequently, when the two parties are making the terms and conditions of the contract, more or less clause may be adopted. If the quality delivered by the seller is within the limitation of contract, this delivery can be considered in compliance with the contract. The buyer cannot refuse to take the delivery. The followings are the two ways often used in practice.

(1) Quality Latitude/ Quality Flexible Allowance

Quality latitude/quality flexible allowance refers to the flexibility for those specific quality indications in a certain range. The following three methods are often used in practice.

a. Specification of range: moisture 5%−10%.

b. Specification of limitation: maximum or minimum, wool 98% min.

c. Specification of more or less: Eiderdown content 16%, 1% more or less.

(2) Quality Tolerance

In trading agricultural products, industrial raw materials or some products of light industry a tolerance clause is usually stipulated in the sales contract. Quality tolerance means the permissible range within which the quality supplied by the seller may be either superior or inferior to the quality stipulated in the contract. The tolerance may be that agreed upon between the seller and the buyer beforehand, or that generally recognized by trade associations. Such tolerance can be compensated by the increase or decrease of the price in proportion to the degree of the tolerance. Sometimes, price adjustment is not needed if the tolerance is within certain limit.

If there is specific and popular quality tolerance for some line or standard for the goods about to be transacted, it is not necessary for this quality tolerance to be stated in the contract. However, if there is no clear or popular "qualitytolerance" for the goods in the world market, or there is no definite understanding of the "quality tolerance" by the seller and the buyer, or there is a need to extend the "quality tolerance" because of production needs, the quality tolerance, in the case, can be specified clearly in the contract. This is the quality tolerance range agreed upon by both parties.

When the allowance of the quality tolerance delivered by the seller or the quality tolerance falls in line with the agreed range, the price of the quality tolerance can be calculated over thecontract. There is no need to make adjustment.

2. Examples in Contract 公差合同示例

The quality clauses in an export contract, in general, include the name, specification or grade standard and brand name, etc. of the subject goods. In the case of sale by sample, the reference number and the sending date should be included; sometimes a brief specification may also be attached. For example:

a. Sample No.210 Man T-Shirt.

b. Brazilian Coffee Beans 2011 New Crop, F.A.Q.

c. Tetracycline HCL Tablets (sugar coated) 250mg B.P. 1993.

d. Cotton Grey Shirting, 30s×36s 72×69 NO. of threads 38"×121. 5yds.

e. Chinese Northeast Rice, Moisture 25% (max), Admixture 0.25% (max).

f. Red Nylon Cloth Umbrellas for Ladies, 18"×8 ribs, Stainless Steel Shaft, Plastic Handles.

Quiz 课后思考题

1. 品质机动幅度可以怎样规定？
2. 什么叫"凭样品买卖"？有哪些方式？
3. 货物品质的表示方法有哪些？
4. 请解释下列术语：统计过程控制、流程图、附加值、投机商。

Chapter Six　Quantity of Goods
第六章　货物数量跟单

在纺织国际贸易中,买卖双方在签订合同时,要对标的物的数量进行约定,这就是"数量条款"。跟单员在开始跟单前,必须认真阅读和理解合同中的数量条款,并正确计算各种原辅料数量,了解国际惯例中该条款的各种术语,如"分批交货""溢短装条款"等,并合理利用国际惯例,生产和出运符合要求的商品数量。

Section One　Calculating Units of the Goods Quantity
第一节　货物数量的计量单位

在纺织国际贸易中,常用的度量衡制度有公制(metric system)、英制(british system)、美制(U.S. system)和国际单位制(international system of units)。我国采用国际单位制,简称 SI 制。各国度量衡制度不同,要求跟单员熟练转换各种计量单位,以符合本国的习惯。本节包含的与纺织品相关的常用计量单位,作为跟单员应熟练掌握。

1.Units of Measurement 计量单位

Any business deal consists of a certain quantity of goods supplied by the seller and a certain sum of money paid by the buyer. Thus, quantity clause is one of the essential terms and conditions for the conclusion of a transaction in the contract. The United Nations Convention on Contracts for International Sale of Goods requires that the quantity of goods delivered should be identical to that called for in the contract, otherwise the buyer is entitled to reject the portion of goods excessive in quantity, and to claim against the seller if the quantity is found to be less than that called for in the contract. If the seller delivers a quantity of goods greater than that required in the contract, the buyer may take delivery or refuse to take delivery of the excess quantity. If the buyer takes delivery of all or part of the excess quantity, he must pay for it at the contract rate.

Because different countries have different systems on units of measurement such as length, capacity and weight. Furthermore, the same unit of measurement may represent different quantities. Take example of "ton". There are various "ton" weighing differently systems such as Long ton/English ton (2240Ibs), short ton/American ton (2100Ibs) and Metric ton/French ton (about 2204Ibs). Therefore, it is greatly important for the traders to know the units of measurement in different systems and the way how they are converted into another. The commonly used systems in the world are the Metric System, the British System and the US System. What unit of measurement should be chosen in the contract should go in accordance with the nature of goods. The units of measurement generally used in international trade are listed in Tab 6.1.

Tab 6.1　Units of Measurement

Type	Units of Measurement
Weight	gram(g), kilogram(kg), ounce(oz), pound(lb), metric ton(M/T), longton (L/T), short ton (S/T), etc.
Number	piece (pc), package (pkg), pair, set, dozen (doz), gross (gr) ream (rm), etc.
Length	meter (m), centimeter (cm), foot (ft), yard (yd), etc.
Area	square meter (m^2), square foot (ft^2), square yard (yd^2), etc.
Volume	cubic meter (m^3) cubic centimeter (cm^3), cubic foot (ft^3), cubic yard (yd^3), etc.
Capacity	liter (L), gallon (gal), pint (pt), bushel (bl), etc.

Tab 6.2–Tab 6.5 are the main measurement conversion often used in international trade practice.

Tab 6.2　Length Conversion

Metric System		Chinese System	Britain/American System		
Meter	Centimete	Chi	Yard	Foot	Feet
1	100	3	1.094	3.2808	39.3701
0.01	1	0.03	0.01094	0.03281	0.3937
0.3333	33.33	1	0.3646	1.094	13.123
0.9144	91.44	2.473	1	3	36
0.3048	30.18	0.9144	0.3334	1	12
0.0254	2.54	0.0762	0.0278	0.0833	1

Tab 6.3　Area Conversion

Metric System		Britain/American System		Chinese System	
Square Meter	Square Centimeter	Square Yard	Square Foot	Square Feet	Square Chinese Meter
1	10000	1.196	10.7639	1550	9
0.0001	1	0.00012	0.00108	0.155	0.0009
0.9361	8361	1	9	1296	7.525
0.0929	929	0.111	1	144	0.836
0.00065	6.45	0.00077	0.00694	1	0.0058
0.111	1111	0.133	1.196	172.2	1

Tab 6.4　Capacity Conversion

Metric System	Chinese System	Britain System	American System
Liter	Chinese Liter	Britain Gallon	American Gallon

Metric System	Chinese System	Britain System	American System
1	1	0.22	0.264
4.546	4.546	1	1.201
3.785	3.785	0.833	1

Tab 6.5   Volume Conversion

Metric System		Britain/American System			Chinese System
Cubic Meter	Cubic Centimeter	Cubic Yard	Cubic Foot	Cubic Feet	Cubic Chinese Meter
1	1000000	1.303	35.3147	61024	27
0.000001	1	0.0000013	0.00004	0.06102	0.000027
0.7636	764555	1	27	46656	20.463
0.02832	28317	0.037	1	1728	0.7646
0.000016	16.387	0.00002	0.00058	1	0.00044
0.037	37037	0.0484	1.308	2260	1

2. Weight Measurements for Textiles 纺织品重量计量

In textile international trade, the methods to measure the weight of goods are stated as follows.

(1) By Gross Weight

Gross weight is the sum of total weight of the commodity itself and the tare (the package weight). That's to say it refers to the net weight plus the tare weight of the goods.

(2) By Net Weight

Net weight is the actual weight of commodity without the addition of the tare. Intextile international trade if the goods are sold by weight, the net weight is often used.

Net Weight = Gross Weight − Tare Weight

There are four ways to calculate tare weight.

a. By actual tare: The actual weight of packages of the whole commodities.

b. By average tare: In this way, the weight ofpackages is calculated on the basis of the average tare of a part of the packages.

c. By customary tare: The weight of standardized package has a generally recognized weight which can be used to represent the weight of such packages.

d. By computed tare: The weight of package iscalculated according to the previously agreed upon by the seller and the buyer instead of actual weight.

It is customary to calculate the weight by net weight if the contract does not stipulate definitely by gross weight or by net weight. Occasionally, the weights of some commodities areusually calculated by conditioned weight and the oretical weight. Commodities with regular specifications and regular sizes, such as galvanized iron and steel plate, are suitable to be weighed by the oretical weight which is computed by the total number of the sheets.

（3）Conditioned Weight

This refers to the kind of weight derived from the process, with which the moisture content of the commodity is removed and standardized moisture added both by scientific methods. This kind of calculating method is suitable to those cargoes, which are of high economic value and with unsteady moisture content (whose water contents are not stable), such as wool, raw silk, etc.

The formula of calculating the conditioned weight is:

$$\text{Conditioned Weight} = \text{Actual Weight} \times (1 + \text{Standard Regaining Rate of Water}) / (1 + \text{Actual Regaining Rate of Water})$$
$$= \text{Dried Weight} + \text{Standard Moisture}$$

（4）Theoretical Weight

Commodities that have regular specifications and fixed regular size, such as galvanized iron, tin plate and armor plate are often subject to the use of theoretical weight. So long as the specifications and the size of such commodities are the same, their theoretical weight is constructed by the number of the sheets put together. Some fixed cargoes, such as tin plate, steel plate, etc have unified shapes and measurement, as long as the specification is identical, the size is conformable, the weight will be about the same, and we can calculate the weight according to the number of pieces.

（5）Legal Weight

Legal weight is the weight of the goods and the immediate package of the goods. Such kinds of goods include cans, small paper boxes, small bottles, etc.

Section Two　Quantity Terms in the Contract
第二节　合同中的数量条款

在纺织品外贸跟单中,成交的商品,如纤维原料、纱线、面料等往往为大宗商品,由于商品自身特点和加工条件限制等因素,实际生产数量与合同规定数量总会有所偏差。对于这类交易,在合同中一般约定卖方可以以某个数量为基准,允许其向上或向下有一定浮动,只要最终商品数量在这个浮动范围之内,即视为卖方达到了交货数量要求。这种针对商品数量的机动幅度条款称为"溢短装"条款,这种条款实际上为卖方履行合同提供了便利。

买卖双方在合同中订立数量条款时,应包括成交商品的数量、计量单位、"溢短装"条款等,在制定数量条款时,注意应当明确具体、合理规定数量机动幅度条款、明确计量单位所采用的度量衡制度以及国际惯例对数量的规定。

1.More or Less Clause 数量条款示例

At the time of the conclusion of a contract, the quantity clause should be clearly and definitely stipulated so as not to give rise to disputes thereafter, expressions like "about" or "approximate 10, 000 metric tons" would not be allowed because "about or approximate" may be given several ambiguous interpretations: some refer to 2% more or less, and some 5%, and some 10%. However, it is very difficult to measure accurately those bulk goods of agricultural and mineral products like corn, soybean, wheat, coal, etc. In some cases, because of the change of goods resources or the imitation of processing, the quantity of the goods last delivered may be not in accordance with the stipulations in the contract. What's more, influenced by natural conditions, packing patterns, loading and unloading methods, the quantity of goods delivered by the seller usually doesn't conform to the quantity definitely stipulated in the contract. In order to facilitate the processing of the contract, the seller and the buyer, generally, agree to use "more or less clause". It means over-load and under-load are permitted but should not surpass a certain percentage of the stipulated quantity. That's to say both the seller and the buyer agrees to allow some more or less of the goods delivered, but not exceeds the fixed quantity agreed upon. For example, 20,000 metric tons, 5% more or less at sellers' option" "plus or minus" or the sign "±" may also be used to take the place of "more or less" under the "more or less" clause, the payment for the over-load or under-load will be made according to the contract price or at the market price at the time of shipment.

A complete more or less term should include the following three parts: First, there is a certain proportion. Secondly, who has the right to decide the more or less term when the goods aredelivered, generally speaking, it is decided by the seller, but when the buyer is responsible for renting the whole ship of the goods, in order to be linked with the charter party, sometimes it can be decided by the buyer. Thirdly, pay attention to the calculation of "more or less clause". Under the "more or less clause" the payment for the over-load or under-load will be made according to the contract price, and it can also be made according to the goods and the market situation at the market price at the time of shipment. If there are no comments on more or less clause, as a usual practice. it can be understood as the payment for the over-load or under-load will be made according to the contract price.

The commonly used examples are stated as follows.

a. 5% more or less in quantity and amount will be allowed.

b. 5 PCT more or less both in amount and quantity per each item will be acceptable.

c. With 10% more or less both in amount and quantity per each item will be acceptable.

d. 5% more or less in amount of credit and quantity of merchandise acceptable.

e. Both amount and quantity plus or minus 5 PCT acceptable.

f. Both quantity and credit amount 10 PCT more or less are allowed.

g. 5% more or less in quantity(QTY) & amount at the seller's option.

h. Amount of credit and quantity of merchandise 5% more or less acceptable.

i. 5% more or less in quantity and invoice value are allowed.

j. Ten PCT more or less in both quantity and credit amount allowed.

k. ±5% in quantity and amount will be allowed.

2.Attentions When Making Quantity Terms

Important points that should be taken into notice when making quantity terms are as follows.

a. Understanding very clearly the whole quantity to be delivered both for import and export.

b. The supply conditions at home market.

c. The supply conditions at abroad market.

d. The financial standing and management capability of the foreign customers.

e. The price fluctuation both at world market and home market.

f. Bleached cotton clothing 25,000 yds, with 5% more or less at seller's option.

g. Chinese northeast soybean: 6,000M/T, gross for net, 3% more or less at sellers' option.

h. 500 metric tons, 5% more or less at seller's option.

i. The seller is allowed to load 3% more or less; the price shall be calculated according to the unit price in the contract.

j. To be packed in double gunny bags containing about 100 kgs and each bag shall weigh 1.15kgs with allowance of 0.1kg more or less.

k. It is agreed that a margin of 10% shall be allowed for over or short count.

l. For printed, dyed and yarn-dyed goods, a maximum of 10% of two-part pieces with the short part not less than 10yds is permissible if necessary and for each two-part pieces an additional length of 1/2 yd (half yard) will be supplied free. Also, a tolerance of plus or minus 10% in quantity for each colorway (for each shade in case of dyed goods) shall be permitted.

m. A usual trade margin of 5% plus or minus of the quantities confirmed shall be allowed. When shipment is spread over two or more periods, the above-mentioned trade margin of plus or minus 5% shall, when necessary, be applicable to the quantity designated by the buyers to be shipped each period.

In order to avoid unnecessary disputes, the quantity terms in the contract should be madevery specific and clear. It is better not to use the words like "about, approximate". This is because there is different understanding for these words, which will cause ambiguity. It should be also very clear for quantity units. For example, if it is calculated by tons, there will be M/T, or L/T, or S/T. For the goods calculated by weight, the specific calculating method should be stipulated, such as "gross for net".

Quiz　课后思考题

1. 在外贸跟单中,重量的确定有哪些方法?
2. 国际贸易中常用的长度单位和重量单位有哪些?
3. 为避免不必要的纠纷,外贸合同中数量条款要注意哪些地方(至少列举 5 条)?
4. 解释下列术语:进口配额、订金、皮重、运输条款、溢短装。

Chapter Seven　Packing of Goods
第七章　包装跟单

　　国际贸易的货物一般情况下都是需要包装的,包装一方面可以保护货物,使其在运输过程中不会受到损伤;另一方面可以提升产品价值,吸引消费者。因此,包装在国际贸易中起到了非常重要的作用,对于跟单员来说,包装跟单也是重要的环节。

　　本章从包装的作用、包装的种类、包装的标志三个方面详细地介绍了包装跟单的要点,此外,由于近几年跨境电子商务的蓬勃发展,因此也单列一节介绍。

Section One　The Function of Packing
第一节　包装的作用

　　包装的功能主要有两方面:一是自然功能,即对商品起保护作用;另一是社会功能,即对商品起媒介作用,也就是把商品介绍给消费者,吸引消费者,从而达到扩大销售、占领市场的目的。这两种功能相辅相成。自然功能保护商品处于完好状态,为社会功能的实现提供可能;社会功能把商品尽快地推向消费者手中,使自然功能得以有效实现。而对于一种商品来说,包装的自然功能和社会功能如何,直接影响该商品在市场中的竞争力。

　　Packing, in business practice, is one of the most important problems that confront the merchants engaged in foreign trade. It needs more care in export trade than domestic trade. The real art of packing is to get the contents into nice, compact shape that will stay in perfect condition with nothing missing during the roughest journey.

　　Packing has become more and more important in competing for overseas markets. One of its basic purposes is to protect the product. This is important because the product may have to withstand a lot of handling during transportation between the factory and the consumer. The second purpose of packaging is to make the product look appealing to the buyer. Products that are packed in such a way as to catch the consumer's eyes will help to sell. Other common purposes of packing are to provide information about the product inside, make it easy to carry the product, and provide convenience using the product. Therefore, more and more people, not only manufacturers, have come to realize the importance of packaging.

1.Problems in Transport 运输中的问题

　　Generally speaking, goods sent by air are usually handled more carefully, although there are occasionally examples of mishap such as goods arriving at the wrong destination or fresh vegetables arriving frozen. During the process of shipment, the packing case in which the export goods traveling may not be properly unloaded from the truck and may in fact be dropped. The crate may suffer from dragging, tumbling and lifting; it may be placed the wrong way up. If the crate is damaged at the stage, it will be vulnerable throughout the rest of its journey to the entry of dirt and to the attention or would-be pilferage. At the stage of loading the goods aboard a ship, slings, grabs and nets used may not be properly located, causing crushing from without and pressures from within. In the ship's hold, the crate may be subject to further dropping, tumbling, leveling or hooking.

During the voyage, the movement of ships may cause fastenings of boxes or crates to become loose, the interior blocking and bracing to be dislocated, the walls of the boxes or crates to beckon punctured, and even some of the markings to become obliterated. The ship's constant movement causes the friction within the hold. When the box or crate is unloaded at the port of destination, stevedores may be illiterate, and unable to read cautionary signs "This Side Up", even if printed in their own language. There may not be adequate covered storage available for the goods, sometimes even no proper unloading equipment. Numerable unexpected problems at any state of the journey mayoccur. If the packing provided by the exporter is proper, sound and strong enough to sustain any rough and improper handling, all these can be avoided considerably.

2.Purpose of Packing 包装的目的

It is because of all the problems that may occur during the transportation that we have to pay great attention to packing. Before goods are packed, exporters should consider about what the purpose of the packing is. In general, there are several objectives facing all the exporters. So they have to make sure what objectives the goods are to be packed.

a. Packing can be used to protect the goods and keep them as good and complete as they are shipped in the circulation field. Generally speaking, only packed commodities can enter into the circulation field, and attain the commercial value and use value of the goods.

b. It makes the commodities convenient for storing, taking care of, transportation, loading, unloading, and calculating them. Cargo packing in design, namely dimension and configuration, should facilitate the most economical method of handling. This is particularly relevant to awkward shaped cargo. Moreover, it applies from the time the goods are packaged, which may be in the factory, until it reaches the importer's warehouse/distribution centre. Mechanical and computerized and high-tech cargo handling equipment is now in extensive use to reduce labor cost and speed up cargo handling.

c. Strong packing can prevent the goods from being stolen and damaged. It can be used to improve standards to reduce risk of damage and pilferage. This in turn encourages competitive cargo insurance premiums and maintains good relations with the importer. Cargo received in a damaged condition seriously impairs the exporter's product overseas market prospects as it loses goodwill with the importer. Moreover, the exporter is ultimately obliged to replace the damaged goods, which can be a costly task.

d. Reasonable packing can lessen shipping space and save freight. Good packing can insure the lowest insurance premium.

e. Marketing packing makes it convenient for consumers to select, carry, or use the goods.

f. Marketing packing can also beautify the commodity, attract consumers, expand sales and increase the gains on foreign exchange.

In addition to all those mentioned above, packing of the goods, in a sense, incarnate the level of a country's economic construction, science and technology, culture and art, etc.

3.Practical Suggestions for Packing Methods 包装方法的实质性建议

There are three steps in export packing. The first step is to determine the hazards involved in shipping the goods to the foreign destination. The second step is to choose the type of box, crate, or container which is most suitable for the goods. Whenever possible, the package should be kept as small and light as you can make it. The third step is to ensure that certain guidelines are observed when the goods are actually packed.

a. Protection from corrosion. Before goods are packed, materials which are liable to deterioration during transit should be properly treated with protection.

b. Protection from damage. Poor packing may result in damage to goods in transit and cause annoyance and inconvenience to customers.

c. Cartons should not be overfilled.

d. Sharp edges on package should be avoided.

e. Measures of security against hazards and pilferage, fire, containerization corporation, etc. should be attended to.

f. Goods like tea must be carefully packed not only against the usually climate perils, but must be also tightly scaled so as to prevent it from absorbing odors and smells from the surrounding cargo.

g. Food articles have to be packed very carefully and in sanitary cans.

h. Cargoes shipped in bulk require little or no packing.

i. As to the highly dangerous materials, the shipping companies do lay down specifications for packages.

j. As for the goods packed by cases, it is better to line with waterproof cloth inside the cases.

4.Factors Influencing Types of Cargo Packing 影响各类货物包装的因素

(1) Value of goods

In the main the high-value consignment usually attracts more extensive packing than the low value merchandise. Much, of course, depends on the nature of the commodity. If packing is inadequate bearing in mind transit and cleared cargo valuation, problems could be experienced in carrier's liability, acceptance and adequate cargo insurance coverage. Moreover, high-value consignments, such as a valuable painting, require adequate security, and likewise attract high freight rate, such packing must be done professionally.

(2)Nature of the transit

The type and the length of transit are another factors that can influence packing. Is the movement national or transglobal? What form of transport will be used during the transit, road, rail, short-sea, deep-sea or air? All have varying characteristics which make varying demands of the packaging of the goods. Furthermore, one must consider the method of shipment, it may be break−bulk, LCL or FCL.

（3）Nature of cargo

This concerns the characteristics of the goods concerned and their susceptibility to various loss/ damage. This factor, together with item （2）, is the two major factors which determine the type of packing for an individual consignment. Cargo shipped in bulk requires little or no packing, while general merchandise needs adequate packing. For example, apples can be consigned in cases, boxes, cartons or pallet boxes. Grain, ores and coal are all shipped in bulk.

（4）Compliance with customs or statutory requirements

This is particularly relevant to dangerous cargoes where strict regulations apply both by air and sea concerning the carriers' acceptance, packing, stowage, documentation, marking and carriers' liability. In the EU stringent regulations exist under the European Packing Waste Legislation of 2001. This embraces a high proportion of packaging to be recovered and recycled after use.

（5）Resale value, if any, of packaging material in the importer's country

In some developing countries, large drum, wooden cases, or bags have a modest resale value. This helps to reduce the packaging cost.

Section Two   Kinds of Packing
第二节   包装的种类

国际贸易的货物包装可以有多种形式,按形态可以分为两大类:一类是散装货物(也称为裸装货物),是指不加包装,基本上以其自然形态装上车、船、飞机等运输工具运送的进出境货物,主要为粮食、矿石、水泥、原油、废钢铁等块状、粒状、粉末状以及液态的大宗货物;另一类是非散装货物,这类货物需要有运输包装和销售包装,大多数货物属于这一类。本节将介绍这两种货物的包装方式。

还可以按对内容物的作用分为运输包装和销售包装,按品牌和产地的标识方式分为中性包装和定牌包装。

1.Nude Cargo, Cargo in Bulk/Bulk Cargo and Packed Cargo 裸装、散装及包装货

The kinds of cargoes are various in international trade, from the view point of whether they need packing, they fall into three kinds.

（1）Nude cargo

Nude cargoes or nude packed commodities refer to those kinds of cargoes whose qualities are more stable and to be shipped without any packages or in simple bundles. They are not easy to be influenced by outside circumstances and they become single pieces of their own. They are difficult to be packed or do not need any packing, such as products, lead ingot, timber, rubber, automobile.

（2）Cargo in bulk/Bulk cargo

Cargo in bulk refers to goods which are shipped or even sold without packages on the conveyance in bulk, such as oil, ore, grain, coal. Cargoes in bulk can be transported, loaded and unloaded by conveyance and loading and unloading equipment designed particularly. Bulk shipment is usually applicable for large quantity of commodities that are to be shipped by means of transport with special purposed shipping equipment. Bulk shipment has the advantages of space saving, quick handling and lower freight.

（3）Packed cargo

Most of commodities in international trade need certain degree of packing during the shipping, storing and sales process. Packed cargoes refer to those which need shipping packing, marketing packing or both.

2. Transport/Shipping Packing and Sales/Marketing Packing 运输包装和销售包装

In international trade, according to the functions of the goods in the process of circulating, and the packing materials and methods, packing can be divided into transport/shipping packing (also called outer packing) and sales/marketing packing (also called inner packing). As Fig 7.1 shows outer packing and inner packing.

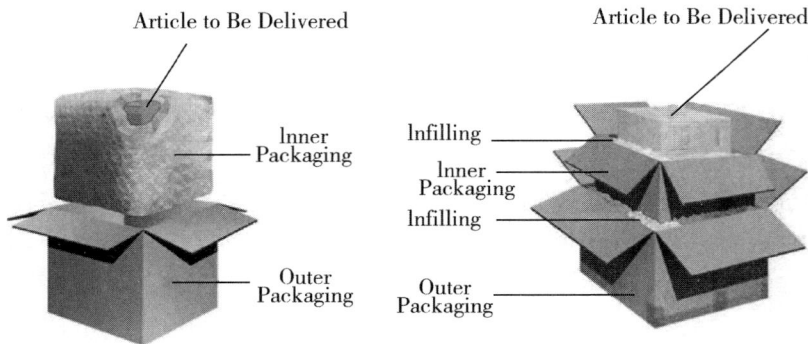

Fig 7.1　Outer Packing and Inner Packing

（1）Transport/Shipping packing (Outer packing)

Transport/shipping packing is also called big packing or outside packing, or outer packing or giant packing. It is used mainly to keep the goods safe and sound during transportation. It must not only be solid enough to prevent the packed goods from any damage, but also be urglarproof, easy to store, convenient to load and unload and discharge. On the basis of packing materials and packing methods, transport packing includes the following types, see Tab 7.1.

Tab 7.1　Types of Packing Containers

Bag	May be made of strong paper, linen, canvas, rubber, etc.
Sack	A lager bag usually made of jute

Continued

Carton	Made of light but strong cardboard, or fiberboard with double lids and bottoms, fixed by glue, adhesive tapes, metal bands or wire staples. sometimes a bundle of several cartons is made up into one package, held by metal bands
Case	A strong container made of wood. Fox extra strength it may have batters. Sometime thinner wood may be used with metal bands or wires passed around the case. The inside of the case may be lined with carious materials, e. g. Damp resisting paper, tin foil, etc. To prevent damage by water, air or insects
Box	A small case, which may be of wood, cardboard or metal, and may have a folding (hinged) lid
Crate	This is a case, but one not fully enclosed. It has a bottom and a frame, sometimes open at the top Crates are often built for the particular things they have to carry. Machinery packed in crates needs a special-bottom (a skid) to facilitate handing
Drum	A cylinder-shaped container for carrying liquids, chemicals, paints, etc. It is usually made of metal. Certain dry chemicals(non-inflammable) or powers are sometimes packed in wood or cardboard drums
Bale	A package of soft goods (e. g. cotton, wool, sheepskin) tightly pressed together and wrapped in a protective material, usually size 30× 15 × 15 inches. May be strengthened by metal bands
Can/Tin	A small metal container in which small quantities of paint oil, or certain foodstuff are packed
Carboy	A large glass container protected in a metal or wicker cage with soft packing between glass andcage. It is used for chemicals
Bundle	Miscellaneous goods packed without a container. A number of small cartons fixed together could be called a bundle
Container	A very large metal box for transport of goods by road, sea or air. Packing goods in large container facilitates loading and unloading by mechanical handling;thus, time is saved
Pallet	A large tray or platform for moving loads (by means of stings) e.g., from, a lorry into a train or onto a ship, so to save time for handling of separate items

(2) Sales /Marketing packing (Inner packing)

Sales/marketing packing (also called inner packing, small packing or immediate packing) is not only adopted as a form of protection to reduce the risks of goods being damaged in transit and prevent pilferage, but mainly with the purpose of promoting sales. It is now universally recognized as a decisive aid in selling household consuming goods. It can be realized in various forms and with different materials as long as it is nice to look at, easy to handle and helpful to the sales. See Fig 7.2. The sales packing can be decided as wholesale package (package) and retail package (small package).

Fig 7.2　Shirt Sales Packaging

3.Neutral Packing and Brand Designated by the Buyer 中性包装和定牌

（1）Neutral packing

The neutral packing means that there is neither a name of the origin, nor a name and address of the factory/manufacturer, nor a trade mark, a brand, or even any words on the (outer or inner) packing of the commodity and the commodity itself. The purpose of using neutral packing by exporters is to break down the tariff and non-tariff barriers of some countries or regions, or to meet the special demand of the transaction (such as entrepot). It mayalso, help the manufacturers in exporting countries to increase the competitiveness of their products, expand the exports and market profitably in the importing countries. It is, sometimes, used as a struggling means to increase market profitable and the competitiveness, and expand sales. At present, using the packing for the marketing packing of some exporting commodities has become somewhat of a practice in international trade. Fig 7.3 shows neutral packing.

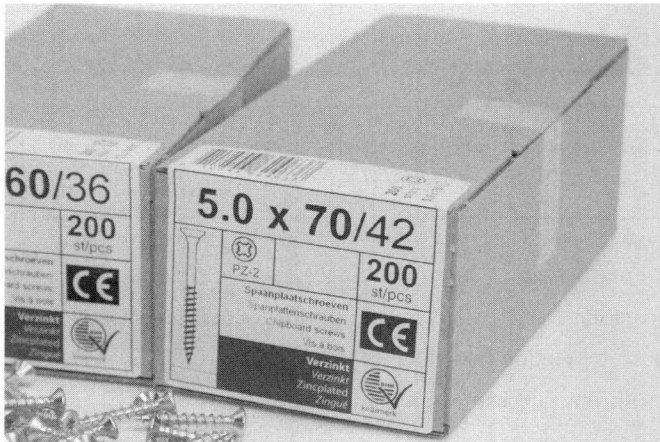

Fig 7.3　Neutral Packing

（2）Brands designated by the buyer

Brands designated by the buyer refer to the packing that the goods should be packed according to the trade marks and brands by the buyer. As to the goods to be ordered regularly in large quantities for a long time by foreign customers, in order to expand sales. we can accept trade marks designated by buyers with indicating the mark of the manufacturing country, that is, the neutral packing with brands designated by the buyers. Sometimes we may accept trade marks or brands designated by buyers from foreigncountries, but under the trade marks and brands, we indicate "Made in the People's Republic of China" or "Made in China". In some other cases, we may accept the designated trade marks or brands and the same time, under the trade marks or brands we indicate that the goods are made by a factory at the buyer's country, i.e., trade marks or brands and origins designated by the buyers.

Section Three   Marking of Package
第三节　包装标志

包装标志是指为了便于货物交接,防止错发错运,便于识别,便于运输、仓储和海关等有关部门进行查验等,也便于收货人提取货物,在进出口货物的外包装上标明的记号。包装标志按功能可分为运输标志、指示性标志和警告性标志。

1.Classification of Marking of Package 包装标志的分类

When talking about transport packing, the packing mark (or marking of package) of course has to be referred to packing mark or recognition mark refers to which are written, printed, or brushed on the outside of the shipping packing in order that it is easy and convenient for goods' loading, unloading, store, inspection and discharge. Package should not be marked with crayons, tags or card. The best method of marking is to stencil the marks on the outside of the package. Some exporters paint the marks with a brush and indelible ink. All in all, mark should be permanent and easily read at a glance. According to the uses of the packing mark, it can be divided into shipping marks, indicative marks, warning marks and supplementary/additional marks (Fig 7.4).

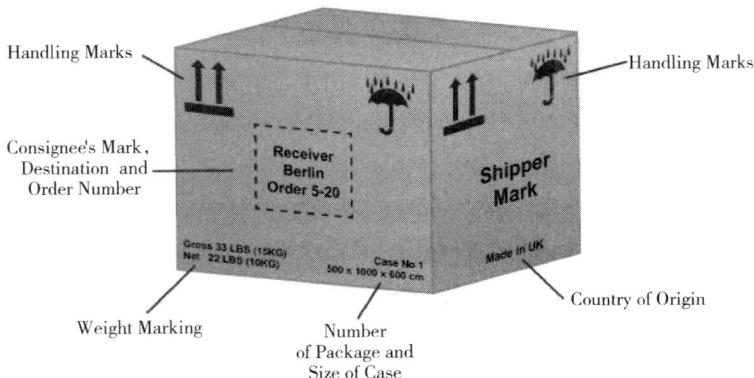

Fig 7.4   Kinds of Packing Marks

2.Shipping Marks 运输标志

Shipping marks are marks of simple designs, some letters, numbers and simple words on packages, often stenciled, that serve as identification of the consignment to which they belong. It is one of the most important elements which are agreed on by the exporter and the importer in a sales contract. The shipping mark consists of name or code of destination, code of consignee or consignor and piece number, serial number, contract number or license number.

An example of shipping marks is illustrated as follows, see Fig 7.5.

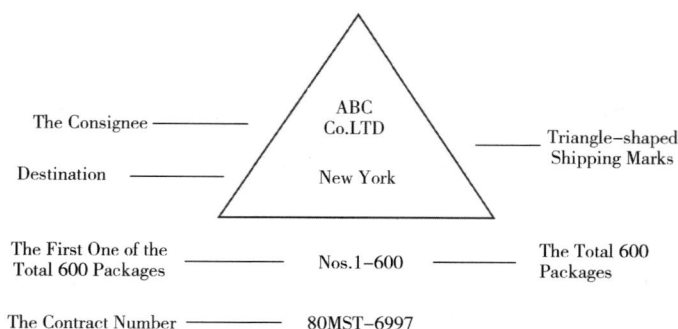

Fig. 7.5 Example of Shipping Marks

Simple shipping marks are generally made up of four parts.

(1) Consignee's code

The consignee's codes are usually indicated by different geometrical diagrams, such as triangles, diamonds, circles, square, etc. With letters inside them as the main marks.

(2) Consignor's code

Letters are usually printed inside or outside the diagrams to represent the consignor's codes.

(3) Name or code of destination

Generally, abbreviated forms or codes are not used to show the destination in order to avoid ambiguity. If there happen to be two same names of different destinations in the world, the name of country must also be printed after the name of the destination in order to avoid wrong delivery.

(4) Package number/Piece number

Below the name of the destination is usually placed the package number. Packages may be numbered consecutively or marked merely with a total number.

3.Indicative Marks 指示性标志

We usually make use of the simple, noticeable design, remarkable diagrams and simple words on the packages to remain the relative workers of the items for attention when they load, unload, carry and store the goods, such as: "HANDLE WITH CARE" "THIS SIDE UP" (Fig. 7.7), etc, which printed in black color generally.

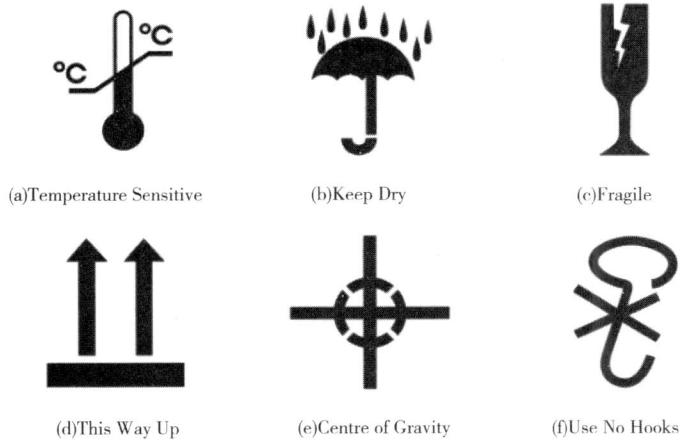

(a)Temperature Sensitive   (b)Keep Dry   (c)Fragile

(d)This Way Up   (e)Centre of Gravity   (f)Use No Hooks

Fig.7.7   Some Indicative Marks

The following are some common markings and phrases:DO NOT DROP, NOT TO BE LAID FLAT, USE NO HOOKS, OPEN HERE, THIS SIDE UP, INFLAMMABLE, NO DUMPING, DO NOT CRUSH, HANDLE WITH CARE, PERISHABLE GOODS, FRAGILE, KEEP FLAT, KEEP DRY.

4.Warning Marks 警告性标志

The warning mark is also called dangerous cargo mark or shipping mark for dangerous commodities, which is brushed/printed clearly and definitely on the shipping packing of the inflammable, explosive, poisonous, corrosive or radioactive goods, so as to give warnings to the workers/dockers/crew.Warning marks are usually made up of simple geometrical diagrams, word descriptions and particular pictures, as to which, every country usually has its own stipulation. For example, our country haspromulgated "Indicative Marks for Packing Storage and Transportation", and "Warning Marks for Packing Dangerous Cargoes". Fig.7.8 shows examples of symbols of warning marks.

Fig.7.8   Examples of Warning Marks

The common warning marks printed on the outer package are:INFLMAHLE COMPRESSED GAS, EXPLOSIVES, CORROSIVES, POISON, MATERIAL RADIOACTIVES, HAZARDOUS ARTICLE, OXIDIIING MATERIAL.

Section Four　Elements Concerning Cross-border E-commodity Packaging
第四节　跨境电子商务商品包装注意要素

　　跨境电商是电子商务的一个分支,近年来的发展势头十分迅猛。由于跨境电商订单小型化、碎片化的特点,货物的包装形式也呈现出一些特殊性。

　　In the era of cross-border e-commerce, merchants tend toaffect the commodity (product) packing design from three aspects: the portection of the goods, the convenience and sales function. Fig 7.9 shows cross-border e-commodity packaging.

Fig 7.9 E-commodity Packaging

1."Special Positioning" for Online Shopping Goods 网购商品的特别定位

　　Now that online shopping has already become a habbit of consumer behavior in the 21st century, occupying more and more market shares, from the stage of packaging at the place of the manufacturers, the feature of online shopping goods should be considered. That means the packaging of online shopping goods should be separated form traditional commodities (off-line) packaging when they are delivered by the factory. So with "special positioning" for online shopping goods, commodity packaging design will be of clear purpose and direction, also avoiding unnecessary charges of packing.

2.The "Function First" Principle"功能第一"原则

　　In e-commerce, customers do goods shopping in a direct contact manner with the goods (image) and instructions about the goods, and thus they do not need to contact packaging or understand the goods from the packaging, therefore, this fails some of functions of the packaging such as the beautification function, the display function, etc. At this point, the commodity packing design principle is "function first". The "function" is mainly refers to the security protection function design, which is separated from "promotion" "beautification" "Show", and other decorative designs. The all−around security of online commodities packaging design includes the security in the aspects of production, transportation, loading and unloading, storage, distribution, as well as in the links of secondary packaging, such as express.

3.Identification of Product and Customer Information 产品和客户信息识别

The currently adopted online packing is mostly plastic bags, corrugated carton, plastic foam box and paper tape, etc. Some packaging like patients, is wrapped in a layer of a layer with adhesive tape paper, with a form almost like from trash. Again, the product information and customer information on the box are with handwritten and copy, which is very vague. Due to the similar size and shape, the same material, the packing bag of approximate colour and lustre, even the courier find it difficult to identify the goods. Customers identify the goods basically based on their memory of the purchase, or else they should open the package to know what's inside. How to use colour and shape of the packing box (bag), mark and clear information program design to better assist the customers identify the goods is a vital issue for cross−border e−commerce.

Quiz　课后思考题

1. 包装的作用有哪些？
2. 国际贸易中,常用的包装种类有哪些？ 常用的包装材料有哪些？
3. 运输标志一般包括哪几部分？
4. 影响包装形式的因素有哪些？
5. 跨境电商商品包装要考虑哪些因素？

Chapter Eight　Delivery of Goods
第八章　货物运输跟单

国际贸易货物的运输是在国家与国家、国家与地区之间货物的运输,它是贸易的重要环节,不仅涉及货物的安全抵达,也涉及货运成本、交货时间、运输保险等相关环节。做好运输跟单,可以确保货物及时安全的交货和货款的及时回收,因此,货物运输跟单也是跟单员的一项重要工作。

Section One　Methods of Delivery
第一节　装运方式

在国际货物运输中,涉及的运输方式很多,其中包括海洋运输、铁路运输、航空运输、河流运输、邮政运输、公路运输、管道运输、大陆桥运输以及由各种运输方式组合的国际多式联运等。各种运输方式各有其优缺点,现将国际贸易中常用的几种方式简略加以介绍。

The delivery of the goods means that the seller delivers the contract goods at the agreed time, place and in the agreed manners to the buyer. In international sales of goods, the delivery also means to transfer the necessary documents at the stipulated time to the buyer. The essentials of a transfer system embrace three elements: the way route, the vehicle (including motive power unit), and the terminal. Each must have a strong interface with the other to generate efficiency and facilitate trade development.

As to the methods of delivery in international trade practice, there are many methods to deliver the goods purchased, such as ocean transport, railway transport, air transport, river and lake transport, postal transport, road transport, pipelines transport, land bridge transport and international multimodal transport and so on. The buyer and seller can decide which method will be the best for goods to be transported according to goods characteristics, quantity, transit journey, value, time, the natural conditions and so on.

1.Ocean Transport 海洋运输

Ocean transport is the most widely used form of transportations in international trade as well as the most efficient form in terms of energy. It still has the attraction of being a cheap mode of transport for delivering large quantities of goods over long distance. Before a shipment is made, the exporter has to consider many different factors influencing the transport considerations such as cost, safety, speed and convenience.

So far as foreign trade is concerned, goods transport is mostly (over 80% of world trade in volume terms) done by ocean vessel. There are several features for ocean transportation: large transport volume, great capability of transport, low freight, sound adaptability to various goods, low speed, high risky.

Because of the prominent advantages over large capability of transport and low freight, the ocean transport still plays a very important role in international transportation even with its low speed and high risks. Nowadays more than 2/3 of transport are done by ocean transportation. There are two kinds of ocean vessels: chartering and liner. Fig 8.1 shows a sea liner.

Fig 8.1　A Sea Liner

(1)Shipping by chartering

Shipping by chartering is also called tramp and it is a freight-carrying vessel which has no regular route or fixed schedule of sailing, or definite freight, or specific port. It is first in one trade and then in another, always seeking those ports where there is a demand at the moment for shipping space. So it is usually used to transport bulk cargo with low value, such as rice, minerals oil and timber, etc. The shipper charters the ship from the ship-owner and uses it to carry the goods. The owner of the cargoes should sign a charter party with the shipper owner. The freight is paid according to the agreement between the two parties.

Shipping by chartering falls into threekinds: voyage charter, time charter and demise charter.

(2)Shipping by liner

A liner is a vessel with regular sailing and arrival on a stated schedule between a group of specific ports. The main features of liners usually includeas:

a. The liner has a regular line, port, timetable and comparatively fixed freight, which is the basic features of liners.

b. The ship-owner usually leases part of shipping space instead of the whole ship.

c. The carrier is responsible for loading and unloading operations, i. e., Gross Terms.

d. The B/L drawn by the shipping company is the shipping contract between the carrier and the consignor. The rights and obligations of the carrier and the consignor are based on the B/L drawn by the shipping company.

2.Railway Transport 铁路运输

Railway transport is capable of attaining relatively high speeds with large quantities and is safe, at low cost, punctual, rather economical and less influence by weather. Railway transport falls into three kinds: domestic railway transport, international railway transport, international railway through transport.

According to the stipulations of the International Union of Railways, the International Railway Cargo Through Transport Agreement and the International Convention Concerning the Carriage of Goods by Rail, the belonging to the export country may be transported directly to the place of destination as long as the canter issues a railway bill of lading at the place of dispatch. Fig 8.2 shows a cargo train.

Fig 8.2　A Cargo Train

The main transport documents are the railway bill and its duplicate. The railway bill is the transportation contract and binding upon the consignee, the consignor and the railway department. The railway bill together with the goods is transported from the place of dispatch to the place of destination and then is delivered to the consignee after he has paid off the freight and other charges. The consignor may make exchange settlement with the bank against the duplicate of railway bill.

3.Air Transport 航空运输

The advantages of air transport are high speed and quick transit, low risk of damage and pilferage with very competitive insurance, saving packing cost, reducing amount of capital tied up in transit and so on; while the chief disadvantage is the limited capacity of air freight and over dimensions of acceptable cargo together with weight restrictions. It is also subject to the influence weather. However, it is suitable those goods that are of time pressing, small quantity of cargoes in urgent need, light but precious. The air transport （Fig 8.3） can be divided into the following kinds：scheduled airliner, charted carrier, consolidation, air express.

Fig 8.3   Air Transport

The airway bill, also called air consignment note, is a document or consignment note used for the carriage of goods by air supplied by the carrier to the consignor. Airway bill has the following features.

a. It is a transport contract signed between the consignor/shipper and the carrier/ airline.

b. It is a receipt from the airline acknowledging the receipt of the consignment from the shipper.

c. The airway bill is an internationally standardized document mostly printed in English and in the official language of the country of departure, which facilitates the on-carriage of goods going through 2 to 3 airlines in different countries to the final destination.

4.Postal Transport 邮包运输

According to international trade practice, the seller fulfills the duty of delivery only if he delivers the parcel to the post office, pays off the postage, and gets the receipt. The post office is responsible for the delivery of the goods to the destination, and the consignee goes to the post office for picking up his goods. Postal transport falls into two kinds：regular mail and air mail.

This method is simple and convenient, and delivery is made simply when a receipt of the goods posted is obtained. It is a kind of international and"door-to-door"transport.According to the postal regulations of the world, the longest length of each parcel limits to one meter, and the weight under 20 kilograms. The restriction of the size and weight on the parcels limits the practicality of this mode, it is only suitable for exactitude instruments, machinery components, bullion ornaments, material medical and other small sized and precious goods. Fig 8.4 shows USPS postal trucks that are loading packages.

Fig 8.4　USPS Postal Trucks

5. International Combined Transport/International Multimodal Transport 国际多式联运

International combined transport means the conveyance of cargo includes at least two modes of transport by which the goods are carried from the place of dispatch to destination on the basis of combined transport or a multimodal transport contract. under this method, the container is used an intemedium and make up of an international multimodal and join transport mode by sea, air and land. It usually includes:

　　a. Train—Air (or Truck—Air, or Ship—Air). The export goods are carried to Hong Kong by train or truck or ship and then loaded into airplanes at Hong Kong.

　　b. Train—Ship. The export goods from Chinese interior provinces may also be transported to Hong Kong by railway for transshipment to foreign ports by vessels.

　　c. Container Transport/Containerized Traffic.

6.Container Transport 集装箱运输

With the expansion of international trade, the container service has become more and more popular, the use of container provides a highly efficient form for transport by ship, by road, by rail and by air though its fullest benefits are felt in shipping, where costs may be reduced by as much as one half. Therefore, nowadays, it has become a very convenient and modem transport method in intenational practice. Containers are constructed of metal and of standard lengths, mostly ranging from ten to forty feet. The International Standard Organization has made 3 catena, 13 classes standard specifications from 1A to 3A, among which the mostly used is Type 1A(8 inches × 8 inches × 840 inches), Type 1C(8 inches × 8 inches × 20 inches) and Type 1AA (8 inches × 8. 6 inches × 40 inches).

　　Container transport falls into two kinds (methods of consignment): full container load (FCL)and less than container load (LCL). As for the consignment that reaches the demand of FCL, the vanning

FCL is done either by the consignor himself or the carrier at the production side or the warehouse, then it is sent to the container yard (CY) for consolidation by the carrier. As for the consignment that does not reach the demand of a full container, we call it less than container, the vanning LCL is done by the consignor himself and then send the consignment to the container freight station (CFS) or inland container depot for consolidation by the carrier, who will piece together the goods according to the nature, destination, weight and so on in the container and then send it to the container yard. Fig 8.5 shows a container yard.

Fig 8.5   Container Yard

7.Land Bridge Transport 大陆桥运输

Land bridge transport is a mode of transport that connects the ocean transport on the two sides of the land by the railway and land which runs across me continent, i. e., ship—train—ship. Land bridge transport uses the container as a medium, so it has an advantage of container transport. There are three main land bridges in the world：①American land bridge；②Siberian land bridge；③The New European—Asia land bridge.

Section Two   Delivery Conditions
第二节   装运条件

装运条件(terms of shipment, delivery conditions)是外贸合同的必有条款,它规定了卖方发货的时间、装运港和目的港、是否允许分批装运和转运、装运通知等要求,跟单员必须全面准确地掌握上述内容。

Delivery conditions, include the time of delivery, and in some cases include the time of loading and unloading, and the charges resulting from loading and unloading operations, the port of shipment, the port of destination, partial shipments and transshipments, shipping documents, etc.

1.Time of Delivery 装运时间

The time of delivery refers to the time limit during which the seller shall deliver the goods to the buyer at the agreed place by the agreed methods. There are the following ways to stipulate the time of delivery in the contract.

（1）Stipulate the definite time of delivery, for example:

a. Shipment on or before March 15th, 2006.

b. Shipment during January/February/March 2006.

c. Shipment on or before April 31st, 2006.

（2）Stipulate a period of fixed time, the seller can arrange shipment during whichever date, for example:

a. Shipment during March 2006.

b. Shipment during January/February/March 2006.

c. Shipment within 15 days after receipt of remittance.

d. Shipment by first available vessel.

（3）Stipulate shipment within...days after receipt of the letter of credit, for example:

a. Shipment within 30 days after receipt of L/C.

b. Shipment within 45 days after receipt of L/C.

c. Shipment within 3 months after receipt of L/C.

（4）Stipulate the goods shall be shipped in the near future, for example:

a. Immediate shipment.

b. Shipment as soon as possible.

c. Prompt shipment.

But there are not unanimous explanations about these terms in the international trade, and thus, it is quiteeasy to result in disputes, so we should try to avoid using them.

2.Port of Shipment and Port of Destination 装运港和目的港

The points that we should pay attention to when stipulating the port of shipment in an export contract.

The port of shipment shall be close to the origin of the goods.

We should take into consideration the loading and unloading, and specific transportation conditions and the standards of freight and various charges at home and abroad.

Under the FOB terms, the buyer is responsible for chartering a ship. However, when we stipulate the port of shipment, the depth of it shall be suitable to the ship chartered by the buyer.

In export trade, it is the usual practice to designate only one port of shipment in one transaction, but exceptionally, when large amounts of goods are involved and, in particular, the goods are stored at different places, two or more ports of shipments are also specified, such as "Shanghai and Guangzhou" "Dalian/Qingdao/Shanghai". Sometimes, as the port of shipment is not yet determined at the time the transaction is being concluded, a general clause like "China ports" may be used.

The port of destination is usually proposed and determined by the buyer, which shall be convenient for reselling the goods and shall be the one at which the vessel may safely arrive and be always afloat. When we determine the port of destination, we must pay attention to the following points.

We should not accept the port in the country with which our government does not permit to do business.

The stipulation on the port of destination shall be definite and specific. We should not use ambiguous terms, such as "main ports in Europe" or "main ports in Africa".

If we have to choose a port which has no direct liner to stop by or the trips are few, we should stipulate "transshipment to be permitted" in the contract.

The port of destination shall be the one at which the vessel may safely arrive and be always afloat as to the business with an inland country. We usually choose a port which is near est to the country. we usually do not accept an inland city as the place of destination unless through combined transportation for which the combined transport operator will be responsible.

3.Partial Shipment and Transshipment 分批装运和转船运输

(1) Definition of partial shipment

In case of an export business covering a large amount of goods, it is necessary to make shipment in several lots by several carriers sailing on different dates.

(2) Reasons for partial shipment

It is done because of the limitation of shipping space available, poor unloading facilities at Me port of destination, dull market season, or possible delay in the process of manufacturing of the goods, etc.

Transshipment in ocean shipping, is the movement of goods in transit from one carrier to another at the ports of transshipment before the goods reach the port of destination.

(3) Reasons for transshipment

Transshipment is necessary when ships sailing direct to the port of destination are not available, the port of destination does not tie along the sailing route of the liner, or the amount of cargo for a certain port of destination is so small that no ships would like to call at that port.

4.Shipping Advice 装运通知

The usual practice of international trade underan FOB term is for the seller, if having got ready for shipment, to send a notice to the buyer before the agreed shipment date (usually 30—45 days before the shipment date), so that the buyer can arrange the relevant vessel for taking the delivery. The buyer, after receiving the relevant notice from the seller, should at the agreed time, notify that seller of the name of the vessel and the estimated arrival date of the vessel. And the seller, after the goods are placed on board the vessel, should at the agreed time, notify the buyer of the contract No. the name and weight of the goods, the invoice amount, the vessel's name and the date of shipments that the buyer can make necessary arrangements for purchasing the relevant insurance and taking delivery of the goods. See Fig 8.6 sample shipping advice.

SHIPPING ADVICE

TO: ISSUE DATE: _____
                                                             OUR REF. DATE: _____

We are Pleased to advice you that the following mentioned goods has been shipped out, full details were shown as follows:

Invoice Number:
Bill of Loading Number:
Ocean Vessel:
Port of Loading:
Date of Shipment:
Port of Destination:
Estimated Date of Arrival:
Containers/Seals Number:
Description of Goods:
Shipping Marks:
Quantity:
Gross Weight:
Net Weight:
Total Value:

Thank you for your patronage. We look forward to the pleasure of receiving your valuable repeat orders.

Sincerely yours,
× × ×

Fig 8.6   Sample Shipping Advice

Section Three   Shipping Documents
第三节   货运单据

货运单据也叫运输单据,是外贸单据中最主要、最核心的一类单据,其中的提单更是物权的象征,它也是交单议付必不可少的单据。在国际货物运输中,货运单据的种类很多,包括海运提单、发票、装箱单、重量单、产地证等,本节重点介绍提单、商业发票和装箱单三种最常用的运输单据。

International trade attaches so great importance to shipping documents that, to a certain degree, it can be called trade of documents, or "symbolic" trade. This is because shipping documents represent the title to the goods. For example, under letter of credit, the buyer cannot take the delivery of the goods until he obtains the shipping documents; on the other hand, only if the seller releases the shipping documents can he receive the payment.

What documents to be used and how to carefully and accurately complete them deserve our adequate attention. As a rule, every contract of sale stipulates the kinds of shipping documents required. Any slightest negligence in these documents might result in serious problems, which is not infrequent in practice. It is, therefore, imperative for both an exporter and an importer to abide by such stipulations. Generally, commercial invoice, bill of lading, insurance policy or certificate, packing list, and weight memo, etc., are called shipping documents.

1.Bill of Lading 提单

(1) What is Bill of Lading

As more than 80 percent of China's exports are carried by sea-going ships, the most important shipping document is the bill of lading. It is a document given by a shipping company, representing both a receipt for the goods shipped and a contract for shipment between the shipping company and the shipper. It is also a document of title to the goods, giving the holder or the assignee the right to possession of the goods. Fig 8.7 showsan example of ocean bill of lading.

(2) Functions of Bill of Lading

The Bill of Lading has three important functions :①It is a receipt for goods signed by the shipping company and given to the shippers. ②It is also evidence of a contract of carriage between the shipping company and shippers. ③It is a document of title because the legal owner of the bill of lading is the owner of the goods. For this reason, the bill of lading can be used to transfer the goods from one owner to another.

(3) Classification of Bill of Lading

There are several types of B/L which are categorized in different ways.

a. On board B/L and received for shipment B/L: according to whether the goods are loaded or not, the B/L can be classified into on board (or shipped) B/L and received (or received for shipment) B/L.

b. Clean B/L and unclean B/L: according to whether there are notes on the B/L, it falls into two kinds: clean B/L and unclean B/L.

c. Straight B/L, order B/L and blank B/L: according to whether the B/L is transferable, it is divided into three kinds: straight B/L, order B/L and blank B/L.

A straight B/L is made out so that only the named consignee at the destination is entitled to take delivery of the goods under the bill. The consignee is designated by the shipper. The carrier has to hand over the cargo to the named consignee, not to any third party in possession of the bill. This kind of B/L is not transferable. The shipper cannot pass the bill to a third party by endorsement. So the bill

MEDITERRANEAN SHIPPING COMPANY S.A., Geneva	ORIGINAL BILL OF LADING
MSC	MSCUDM213932

IS IT PORT-TO-PORT SHIPMENT ? (Fill-in Boxes 7 & 8) Tick ->	X	COMBINED TRANSPORT SHIPMENT ? (Fill-in Boxes 5, 6, 9 & 10) Tick ->	N° of original BoL (number & words) **THREE (3)**	N° of BoL Rider Pages (number & words)

(1) SHIPPER: (Full details)	(2) CONSIGNEE: (Not Negotiable unless «To Order of …»)
EXXONMOBIL CHEMICAL ASIA PACIFIC (A DIVISION OF EXXONMOBIL ASIA PACIFIC PTE LTD)1 HARBOURFRONT PLACE, NO. 06-00 HARBOURFRONT TOWER ONE, SINGAPORE 098633	TO ORDER

(3) NOTIFY: (No responsibility shall attach to Carrier or to his Agent for failure to notify)	(4) SPACE FOR **CARRIER'S AGENTS** ENDORSEMENTS (FCL/FCL, SLSC)
GANSU JIARONG PLASTICS CO., LTD. NO. 1 BEIJIAO DEVELOPMENT ZONE, DUNHUANG, GANSU, CHINA TEL: 86-937-8824451 FAX: 86-937-8822399 ATTN: MS. GAO	POST CODE: 736200

(5) PRE-CARRIED BY: (Combined Transport only) XXXXXXXXXXXXX	(6) PLACE OF RECEIPT: (Combined Transport only) DAMMAM, SAUDI ARABIA
(7) PORT OF LOADING: DAMMAM, SAUDI ARABIA	(8) PORT OF DISCHARGE: XINGANG, CHINA
(9) PLACE OF DELIVERY: (Comb. Trans. only) XXXXXXXXXXXXX	(10) MODE OF ON-CARRIAGE: (Comb. Trans. only) XXXXXXXXXXXXX
(11) VESSEL & VOY. N° MSC ILARIA V. 00281R	(12) AGENTS AT PORT OF DISCHARGE / DELIVERY:

(14) CARRIER'S RECEIPT (Continued on attached Bill of Lading Rider page(s), if applicable)	(13) All details shown in Box 13 are furnished by the Shippers, being their Memoranda. Quantity, Condition, Contents and all other information shown in Box 13 are unknown to the Carrier, who has no means to verify their correctness and does not acknowledge them. The statements of the Shippers in Box 13 do not engage the Carrier contractually or in any other manner.

Identity Marks of Cont. or other packages and seal number(s)	Corresp. number of cont. or other packgs	Total nbr of ctrs or other packgs received by the carrier	Haz Code	Cargo Description (Continued on attached Bill of Lading Rider page(s), if applicable)	Cargo Gross weight	Measurement
SHIPPER'S LOAD,	STOW &	COUNT &	SEAL	2 X 40' CONTAINERS SAID TO CONTAIN AND WEIGH :		
				1980 BAGS LOADED ONTO 36 SHRINK WRAPPED PALLETS EXXONMOBIL LD150AC LDPE SO NO: 2306718	TOTAL 50802 KGS	
CNTR : MSCU 9637640 SEAL : 02887 CNTR : TTNU 5582129 SEAL : 02947						
				FCL/FCL FREIGHT PREPAID SAY : TWO CONTAINERS ONLY		

(15) FREIGHT & CHARGES («PAYABLE» signifies INTENTION. Cargo shall not be delivered unless Freight & Charges are paid)					
Specification of Freight & Charges		Basis	Rate	PAYABLE at	
				POL	POD	ELSEWHERE

SHIPPER'S LOAD, STOWER AND COUNT
Said to contain, the carrier had no means to verify shippers' representation and the latter to be ultimately responsible for shortage established at destination in case the container is discharged with the same seal as noted on this bill of lading.

MEDITERRANEAN SHIPPING CO. (H.K.) LTD.

AS AGENTS FOR THE CARRIER
MEDITERRANEAN SHIPPING COMPANY S.A. GENEVA

| Ad Valorem charges | | | | | |
| Declared value: | | TOTAL FREIGHT & CHARGES | | | |

IN ACCEPTING this BoL, the Merchant expressly agrees to be bound by all the terms, conditions, limitations and exceptions, whether printed, stamped or written hereon and on Page 1, and in particular agrees that the Carrier shall have the right, at its sole discretion, to stuff cargo in containers and to carry on deck containers of all kinds including trailers, tanks, flats, canvas top, pallets, vehicles and boats or similar articles used to consolidate goods.
RECEIVED FOR SHIPMENT in apparent external good order and condition the containers, packages, units bearing the marks and/or numbers shown in Box 14, said to contain the quantity of goods, weights and measurements stated by Shippers in Box 13, which particulars the Carrier has neither checked nor verified.
IN WITNESS whereof, the no. of Original Bills of Lading shown at the top right corner of this contract have been signed. If this is a negotiable (To Order) BoL, the goods will only be delivered if one original BoL, properly endorsed by the Shippers and/or by the bare consignee (and not by the Notify Party), is surrendered, the others to be considered null and void.

PLACE AND DATE OF ISSUE HONG KONG 26-MAY-2008	SHIPPED ON BOARD 26-MAY-2008 DATE	SIGNED ON BEHALF OF THE MASTER MSC AGENT

181

090197 **B**

Fig 8.7   Sample Bill of Lading

is of very restricted application. When the goods are shipped on a non-commercial basis such as samples or exhibits, materials in aid of other countries, or when the goods are extremely valuable, a straight B/L is generally issued.

An order B/L indicates that the bill is made out to the order of or to order of... Any person named in such a bill, which may be transferred/negotiated after endorsement. So it is sometimes called transferable B/L. It is because of this that nowadays, it is commonly used in international practice.

A blank B/L is also called open B/L or bearer B/L. It refers to the bill in which the name of a definite consignee is not mentioned. The area in B/L calling for the name of the consignee is left blank, with neither the name of the consignee nor the phraseology of "to order" filled in. This kind of B/L can be transferred/negotiable without endorsement. There usually appear in the box of consignee words like "to bearer" and holder of the B/L can take delivery of the goods against the surrender of B/L, i. e., ownership of the goods passes when the bill is handed over to anyone.

2. Commercial Invoice 商业发票

(1) Definition of Commercial Invoice

An invoice is a statement sent by the seller to the buyer giving particulars of the goods being purchased, and showing the sum of money due. Different parties require such statements for different purposes.

There are various invoices, such as commercial invoices, banker's invoices, consular invoices, customer invoices and proforma invoices. Among these, the commercial invoice is the most common one and has to be provided for each and every consignment as one of the documents evidencing shipment. Fig 8.8 shows an example commercial invoice.

(2) Functions of Commercial Invoice

The invoice functions mainly as a record of the export transaction for buyers, sellers and customs authorities. Copies of the invoice are used by the exporters, their bank, the paying bank, the receiving agents at the port of discharge, the customs in the exporting country and the importers. The importer needs it to check up whether the goods consigned to him are in compliance with the term and conditions of the respective contract. The banks need it together with the bill of lading and the insurance certificate to effect payment. The customs need it to calculate duties, if any. The exporters and importers need it to keep their accounts. In the absence of a draft, the commercial invoice takes its place for drawing money.

3. Packing List

Packing list is a document made out by a seller when a sale isconcluded in international trade. It shows numbers and kinds of packages being shipped, total of gross, legal and net weights of the packages, and marks and numbers on the packages. It is used to make up the deficiency of an invoice. It also enables the consignee to declare the goods at customs office, distinguish and check the goods

| Issuer　　　　(2)

GUANGDONG TEXTILES IMP. & EXP.
KNITWEARS COMPANY LIMITED
15/F., GUANGDONG TEXTILES MANSION
168 XIAO BEI ROAD GUANGZHOU CHINA | 广 东 省 纺 织 品　　（1）
进 出 口 针 织 品 有 限 公 司
GUANGDONG TEXTILES IMP. & EXP.
KNITWEARS COMPANY LIMITED
15/F., GUANGDONG TEXTILES MANSION
168 XIAO BEI ROAD GUANGZHOU CHINA |

商业发票
COMMERCIAL　INVOICE

No.　　(5) YSM1999B	Date　　(6) OCT.05, 1997
S/C No.　　(7) GD – 98TX2509	L/C No.　　(8) 524250
Terms of payment　　　　(9) BY L/C	

To　　　　(3)

JOHNSON'S S.A.
NUBLE1034
SANTIAGO
CHILE

Transport details　　　　(4)

FROM:　　HUANGPU
W/T:　　　HONG KONG
TO:　　　SANANTONIO.
VESSEL:

Marks and numbers	Number and kind of packages; Description of goods	Quantity	Unit price	Amount
(10)	(11)	(12)	(13)	(14)
JOHNSON'S 97KCS05107 SAN ANTONIO CHILE NO.1 – 80 MADE IN CHINA	GARMENTS (100% COTTON JERSEY BABY'S OVERALL)	4 000PCS	USD1.50/PC	USD6 000.00
JOHNSON'S 97KCS05111 SAN ANTONIO CHILE NO.1 – 80 MADE IN CHINA	GARMENTS (100% COTTON JERSEY BABY'S BEATLE WITH SNAP WITH A SMALL EMB ON NECK)	4 000PCS	USD1.60/PC	USD6 400.00

(15)　　CFRC3% SAN ANTONIO...USD12 400.00
　　　　LESS C3　　　　　　　USD372.00

CFR　SAN ANTONIO　USD12 028.00

TOTAL QUANTITY: 8 000PCS PACKING: 160CARTONS
TOTAL WEIGHT: NET WT.: 1 000KGS　　　GROSS WT.: 1 200KGS
TOTAL: U. S. DOLLARS TWELVE THOUSAND AND TWENTY – EIGHT ONLY.

(16)
WE CERTIFY THAT ALL THE SHIPPED GOODS ARE OF CHINESE ORIGIN.

Fig 8.8　Example of Commercial Invoice

when they arrive at the port of destination, thus, facilitates the clearance of goods through customs. What's more, packing lists can facilitate settling insurance claims in case of loss or damage. Fig 8.9 shows a sample of packing list.

上海进出口贸易公司
SHANGHAI IMPORT & EXPORT TRADE CORPORATION
1321 ZHONGSHAN ROAD SHANGHAI CHINA

PACKING LIST

TEL: 0512-6578876   INVOICE NO.: XH051111
FAX: 0512-6578877   DATE: DEC.02,2007
E-mail: LUZHENSH@163.COM   S/C NO.: TXT07081
        TO: FUJIYAMA TRADING CORPORATION   SHIPPING MARK
        121,KAWARA MACH OSAKA JAPAN   N/M

CASE NO.	GOODS DESCRIPTION & PACKING	QUANTITY (PCS)	G.W (KGS)	N.W (KGS)	MEAS (M³)
1-600 601-1400	DOUBLE OPEN END PANNER 8×10MM(MTM) 10×12MM(MTM) PACKED IN 1 400 CARTONS OF 100 PCS EACH（ONE 20' CONTAINER）	60 000 80 000	1 200 2 000	1 080 1 760	12 8
TOTAL:		140 000	3 200	2 840	20

SAY TOTAL: ONE THOUSAND FOUR HUNDRED CARTONS ONLY.

SHANGHAI IMPORT & EXPORT TRADE CORPORATION
× × ×

Fig 8.9   Sample of Packing List

Section Four   Logistics Mode of Cross-border E-commerce
第四节   跨境电子商务的物流模式

跨境电商的快速崛起促进了跨境电商物流的发展,目前,跨境电商物流有五种模式:国际快递、邮政小包、海外仓、国内快递的跨国业务和专线物流,每种模式有其各自的特点和适用场合。

Currently, there are five kinds of modes for cross-border e-commerce logistics operation as follows: express, postal packets, overseas warehouse, special Courier, central railway multimodal transport. More and more cross-border logistics have adopted "cross-border e-commerce + overseas warehouse" mode, namely, the overseas buyers (enterprises) firstly complete online purchase of products through cross-border e-commerce sites, and then the sellers use their global layout in the localization overseas warehousing, logistics system to realize the goods transportation, and effect delivery in time.

1.The International Express 国际快递

International express is mainly referring to UPS, Fedex, DHL and TNT. The four giants headquarters including UPS and Fedex located in the United States, DHL headquarters in Germany, TNT based in the Netherlands. International express has a very high demand of delivery of information, collection and management, supported by global self-built network and international information systems.

2.The Postal Parcel 邮政小包

The postal network has a global coverage, wider than any other logistics channels. And the postal is commonly state-run, enjoying national tax subsidies, so the price is very cheap. Generally, that the goods are wrapped in a personal way is not convenient for the customs statistics, also leading to failing to enjoy general export tax rebates. At the same time, the postal is slower with high rate of packet loss.

3.Overseas Warehouse 海外仓

Overseas warehousing service refers to logistics service providers, independently or jointly, provide the goods storage, sorting, packing, controlling and management of one-stop service, by the network trading platform in foreign trade, to the seller in a sales target. The seller tends to store the goods in a local warehouse so that when the buyer has a demand, he can make a quick response in a timely manner. The sorting, packaging, and delivery of the goods tend to be dealt with prompt response. Fig 8.10 shows an overseas warehouse in the US. The whole process includes three parts, namely, the initial transportation, warehouse management and local distribution.

4.Multinational Business of Domestic Express 国内快递的跨国业务

EMS is relatively mature, and it can reach more than 60 countries around the world. SF express also has established the express service to the United States, Australia, South Korea, Japan, Singapore, Malaysia, Thailand, Vietnam and other countries, and cross-border B2C service is launched between China and Russia.

5.Special Line Logistics 专线物流

Cross-border railway logistics refers to the transport of goods to abroad by aviation package module, followed by the domestic delivery destination countries through cooperation company, which is

Fig 8.10   An Overseas Warehouse in the US

one of the more popular ways of logistics. Special line logistics can concentrate large quantities of goods to send to the destination, by means of economies of scale to reduce costs, therefore, cheaper than commercial courier, faster than the postal packets, with a low packet loss rate. Compared with the postal packets, the freight cost is high, and the scope of domestic coverage area needs to be expanded.

Quiz   课后思考题

1. 海洋运输有哪些特点？
2. 运费的计算方法有哪些？分别适用于什么场合？
3. 合同或信用证中对装运时间的规定有哪几种常用方法？
4. 提单的作用有哪些？
5. 跨境电商物流有哪些模式？分别适用于什么场合？

Chapter Nine　Transportation Insurance
第九章　运输保险跟单

　　国际货物运输保险,是以对外贸易货物运输过程中的各种货物作为保险标的的保险。为了防止货物在运输过程中发生风险给买卖双方带来巨大损失,大多数情况下都需要给货物投保。外贸货物的运送有海运、陆运、空运以及通过邮政送递等多种途径,跟单员应熟悉保险种类、保险金额与保费的计算、保险合同主要条款等知识。

Section One　Risks, Losses and Expenses
第一节　风险、损失和费用

　　由于海运是国际货物运输的主要形式,绝大多数的纺织品也是通过海运方式出运,本节介绍国际货运海上运输过程中可能发生的各种风险、损失的种类以及产生的各种费用。

　　In international buying and selling of goods, there are a number of risks, which, if they occur, will involve traders in financial losses. For instance, cargoes in transit may be damaged due to breakage of packing, clash or fire. etc. These hazards, and many others, may be insured against. Every year, a certain amount of cargo was destroyed or damaged by perils of the sea in transit, but whichever particular cargo it would be it can not be anticipated. All cargo owners take the risk of loss through the perils. However, foreign traders can insure themselves against many of these risks. Based on the principle that the fortunate helps the unfortunate, the industry of insurance has been developed to overcome these financial losses. Insurance is a process for spreading risk, so that the burden of any loss is borne not by the unfortunate individual directly affected but by the total body of person under consideration. In return for a payment known as a premium paid by the insured, an insurance company will agree to compensate the insured person in the event of losses during the period of insurance.

　　According to the loss or damage caused by risks included in different coverage and the expenses involved, the insurance company is responsible for indemnifying the insured goods. Obviously, risk, loss and expenses are closely related to each other. In order to have a clear understanding of the contents of insurance, these three terms should be clarified.

1.Risks 风险

　　While the cargo traveling to another country, it is likely to encounter various perils which may cause the goods to suffer loss of one kind or another. Marine risks in connection with cargo in transit can be classified into two types: perils of the sea and extraneous risks. Perils of the sea are caused by natural calamities and fortuitous accidents; the latter, by various extraneous reasons, including general extraneous risks and special extraneous risks.

　　(1)Perils of the sea

Perils of the sea are those caused by natural calamities and fortuitous, they mainly include the followings.

a. Natural calamities: disasters such as vile weather, thunder and lighting, tsunami, earthquake, floods, etc. Fig 9.1 shows a sinking cargo ship reported in 2019.

b. Fortuitous accidents: accidents such as ship stranded, striking upon the rocks, ship sinking, ship collision, colliding with icebergs or other objects, fire, explosion, ship missing, etc.

Fig 9.1   A Sinking Cargo Ship

(2) Extraneous risks

Extraneous risks are risks caused by extraneous reasons, consisting of general extraneous risks and special extraneous risks.

a. General extraneous risks include theft or pilferage, rain, shortage, contamination, leakage, breakage, train of odor, dampness, heating, rusting hooking, etc.

b. Special extraneous risks include war risks, strikes, non-delivery of cargo, refusal to receive cargo, etc.

2.Loss 损失

Marine losses are the damages or losses of the insured goods incurred by perils of the sea. Losses sustained by the insured because of the risks listed above come from not only the loss of the goods or the damage done to the goods, but also from the expenses the insured sustained in rescuing the goods in danger. According to the extent of damage, losses in marine insurance fall into two types: total loss and partial loss. The former may be subdivided into actual total loss and constructive total loss; the latter, general average and particular average.

(1) Total loss

Total loss refers to the loss of the entire shipment caused by the occurrence of one of the perils of the sea, fire, or some other reasons.

a. Actual total loss: the actual total loss occurs where the insured goods have been toally lost or damaged, or found to be totally valueless on arrival.

b. Constructive total loss: it is found in the case where an actual total loss appears to be unavoidable or the cost to be incurred in recovering reconditioning the goods together with the forwarding cost to the destination named in the policy would exceed their value on arrival.

（2）Partial loss

Partial loss refers to the loss of part of aconsignment. According to different causes, partial loss can be either general average or particular average.

a. General average. In the insurance business the term "average" simply means loss in most cases. It all goes back to the situation where a ship is in danger, and somebody's cargo has to be abandoned. Whose should it be the captain has to decide, and one of the shippers will suffer. To cover this situation the concept of general average was introduced. It means that whichever shipper loses all or part of his cargo, all the others will club together to recompense him for his loss. All policies the insured take out automatically cover them against it.

b. Particular average. A particular average means that a particular consignment is suffered by one whose goods are partly lost or damaged. When there is a particular average loss, other interests in the voyage (such as the carrier and other cargo owners whose goods were not damage) do not contribute to the partial recovery of the one suffering the loss. An example of a particular average occurs when a storm or fire damages part of the shipper's cargo and no one else's cargo has to be sacrificed to save the voyage. The cargo owner whose goods were damaged asks his insurance company for payment, provided, of course, his policy covers the specific type of loss suffered.

Since most of losses encountered by shippers are partial, that is, of the particular average nature, it is important to know exactly what provisions for such partial losses are in the insurance policy.

3.Expenses 费用

Losses sustained by the insured because of the risks come from not only the loss of the goods or the damage done to the goods, but also from the expenses the insured sustained in rescuing the goods in danger. Transportation insurance not only insures the losses caused by risks but also the losses of expenses. The main expenses include the followings.

（1）Sue and labor expense

These expenses are the expenses arising from measures properly taken by the insured, the employee and the assignee, etc. for minimizing or avoiding losses caused by the risks covered in the insurance policy. The insurer is held responsible to compensate for such expenses.

（2）Salvage charges

Salvage charges are expenses resulting from measures properly taken by a third party other than the insured, the employee and the assignee, etc.

Section Two   Insurance Coverage, Value and Premium
第二节   保险险别、保险金额和保险费

作为跟单员,不仅要了解风险、损失的种类,也要了解保险险种及保险金额和保险费的计算,能够在投保时选择合适的险种。本节主要介绍中国人民保险公司海上保险的三个主要险种及其附加险,以及保费的计算。

The object of buying insurance is to buy as much protection as it is necessary, at as low price as possible. To do this, one has to know what risks can be covered, and to decide how much coverage is needed.

According to People's Insurance Company of China Ocean Marine Cargo Clauses, the insurance is mainly classified into two groups: basic insurance coverage and additional insurance coverage. The applicant can purchase basic insurance coverage individually. However, before purchasing an additional insurance coverage, he has to purchase a basic insurance coverage.Basic insurance coverage is further classified into the following three conditions: free from particular average (F.P.A.), with particular average (W.P.A.) and all risks. The F.P.A. covers mainly total loss and general average, while the W.P.A. covers particular average in addition. The all risks cover, in addition to the scope of W.P.A., such as extraneous risks, shortage risk, intermixture and contamination risk, leakage risk, clash and breakage risk, taint of odor risk, sweating and heating risk, hook damage risk, rust risk, breakage of pacing risk, etc. In case of F.P.A or W.P.A., one or several kinds of these extraneous risks may be covered in addition.

1.Basic Insurance Coverage 基本险

(1) Free from particular average (F.P.A.)

Free from particular average, basically, is a limited form of cargo insurance covering as much as that no partial loss or damage is recoverable from the insurers unless that actual vessel or craft is stranded, sunk or burnt. Under the latter circumstances, the F.P.A. cargo policy holder can recover any losses of the insured merchandise which was on the vessel at the time as would obtain under the more extensive W.P.A. policy. The F.P.A. policy provides coverage for total losses and general average emerging from actual "marine perils".

(2) With average/With particular average (W.A./W.P.A.)

This insurance covers wider than F.P.A. Aside from the risks covered under F.P.A. conditions as above, this insurance also covers partial losses of the insured goods caused by heavy weather, lightning, tsunami, earthquake and/or flood.

(3) All risks

The cover of all risks is the most comprehensive of the three. Aside from the risks covered under F.P.A. and W.P.A. conditions as above, this insurance also covers all risks of loss of or damage to insured goods whether partial or total, arising from external causes in the course of transit. It should be noted that "all risks" does not, as its name suggests, really cover all risks: the "all risks" clause excludes coverage against damage caused by war, strikes, riots, etc. These perils can be covered by a separate clause. And it covers only physical loss or damage from external causes.

2.Additional Insurance Coverage 附加险

According to the nature of goods insured, the cargo may choose any of the three covers mentioned above. If more protections are needed, he may further insure his goods against one or several additional risks. No additional risks can be purchased to insure goods independently. Additional risks include general additional risks and special additional risks. Since the scope of cover of general additional risks is already included into that of all risks, it is not necessary for the goods to be insured by additional risks if it is insured by all risks.

3.Choosing the Right Coverage 选择适当的险别

The clear distinction among the clauses F.P.A., W.P.A. and all risks is of great practical significance. It may help exporters choose the right coverage.

Most exporters will probably want to have the widest form of coverage they can get "all risks" coverage. But because of the nature of their goods, underwriters may agree to provide only a more limited form of cover. Moreover, even though an exporter can get "all risks" coverage, he may well decide that it is uneconomical. An experienced exporter will come to know the losses he can expect, and may find it cheaper to write them off as trade losses than to pay the relatively high all risk premium.

Products should be insured in the appropriate category. A good rule of thumb is that an exporter should insure for the coverage accepted in his particular trade. Now let's examine which type of insurance cover an intelligent exporter would choose for the following items.

a. A consignment of shoes.

b. Logs of wood.

c. Wooden toys.

d. Heavy machinery.

e. Plywood.

f. Bicycles.

Probably, you will give the following answers: a, c, d and f would probably be insured all risks because they are prone to be damaged in transit. Most manufactured goods fall into this category. b would be insured F.P.A., for while it could be lost it is not likely to be damaged, on the other hand, would be insured W.P.A. because it could be damaged in transit, but is less prone to damage than the finished products mentioned. Normally the insurance company will advise the exporter in this respect.

4.Insurance Value and Insurance Premium 保险金额与保险费

(1) Insurance value

Insurance value, in marine cargo insurance, is the actual value of the insurable cargo. It is generally calculated as: Insurance Value = Cost of Goods + Amount of Freight + Insurance Premium +

Percentage of the Total Sum to represent a reasonable profit for the buyer. Insurable value is the maximum amount payable by the insurance company in case of loss and premium is calculated and paid on the basis of this amount.

（2）Insurance premium

The insurance premium is payable to the insurer when he issues the insurance policy or certificate. The premium charge for the insurance policy is calculated according to the risks involved. A policy that protects the holder against limited risks charges a low premium, and policy which protects against a large number of risks charges a high premium. The most frequently used trade terms which affect insurance arrangements are FOB, CFR, and CIF. Where the contract between the exporter and the foreign importer is FOB contract, it is the importer's responsibility to insure the goods. If the goods are contracted to be sold on CIF term, then it is the exporters turn to take out the policy and pay the costs of insurance.

Section Three　Forms of Marine Insurance Contract
第三节　海运保险合同种类

海上货物运输保险合同是指被保险人支付保险费,由保险人按照合同规定的承保范围,对被保险人遭受保险事故造成保险标的的损失以及产生的责任进行赔偿的合同。

海上货物运输保险合同是被保险人与保险人签订的具有法律约束力的书面协议,海上货物运输保险合同的当事人主要包括保险人、投保人、被保险人。海运保险合同也有多种形式,如保险单、保险凭证、预约保单、联合凭证等,其中保险单最常用。

An insurance policy or an insurance certificate is issued when goods are insured. An insurance policy (or a certificate) forms part of the chief shipping documents. A policy also functions as collateral security when an exporter gets an advance against his bank credit.

1.Insurance Policy 保险单

Insurance policy, issued by the insurer, is a legal document setting out the exact terms and conditions of an insurance transaction— name of the insured, the name of the commodityinsured, the amount insured, the name of the carrying vessel, the precise risks covered, the period of cover and any exceptions there may be. It also serves as a written contract of insurance between the insurer and the person taking out insurance (Fig 9.2).

2.Insurance Certificate 保险凭证

Insurance certificate is a kind of simplified insurance policy. The insurance certificate only indicates the name of the insured, name of the insured cargo, quantity, mark, conveyance, place of shipment, place of destination, insurance cover, and insurance amount. But the rights and obligations of two parties are omitted. The insurance certificate has the same legal validity as the insurance policy.

3.Open Policy 预约保单

This type of policy is of great importance for export business, it is convenient method for insuring

CARGO INSURANCE POLICY

(210-Branch)

Issue Time: 26-01-2015 09:43

Agency No	Policy No	Supplement / Application No	Renewal No	Risk No	Issue Date	Period of Insurance Inception Date	
1039	21015000044	0 / 0	0	1	26-01-2015	23-01-2015	

Insured

Name, Surname/Title	:	TO THE ORDER OF BANK AL BILAD		
Address	:	TRADE FINANCE CENTRE TALHIA STREET JEDDAH SAUDI ARABIA TEL,00966-2-610-9035 ATTN,MR. ASHRAF AL		
Identification No	:	5458	Phone :	email :

Policy Holder

Name, Surname/Title	:	TO THE ORDER OF BANK AL BILAD
Identification No	:	TRADE FINANCE CENTRE TALHIA STREET JEDDAH SAUDI ARABIA TEL,00966-2-610-9035 ATTN,MR. ASHRAF AL
Address	:	-

Risk Information

SUM INSURED	USD 14.073,28	% OF INCREASE	10 %
TOTAL SUM INSURED	USD 15.480,61	EXCHANGE RATE	2.3379
PLACE OF DEPARTURE	AMBARLI TURKSIH SEA PORT /TURKEY	PLACE OF ARRIVAL	JEDDAH SEAPORT /SAUDI ARABIA
TYPE OF CONVEYANCE	VESSEL	NAME OF VESSEL	ASTRID SCHULTE
DATE OF LOADING	23-01-2015		

Scope of Cover	Sum Insured(TL)	Rate(%)	Net Premium(TL)
ALL RISKS	36.192,11	0,1250	45,24
WSRCC	36.192,11	0,1000	36,19
	NET PREMIUM		81,43
	GROSS PREMIUM		81,43
	EQUIVALENT TO		USD 34.83

POLICY COVERAGE

Below mentioned coverages are provided by this policy

All Risks, Wsrcc

NOTES / REMARKS

L/C NUMBER:IM1430099
B/L NO:TRIST0267
THE NAME OF ISSUING BANK:BANK AL BILAD, SAUDI ARABIA
THE DATE OF ISSUING OF THE LETTER OF CREDIT: 28.0CTOBER.2014
THIS POLICY COVERING WAREHOUSE TO WAREHOUSE, ALL RISKS, WSRCC, T P AND D, TRANSHIPMENT CLAUSES.
WAR AND STRIKES COVER
SCOPE OF COVERAGE AND SPECIAL CONDITIONS
This policy is based on the proposal and declaration of the Assured or the Insurant; it covers loss and damages arising from the risks within the framework of the attached booklet of General Conditions certified by the ministry and the Special Conditions and clauses stated inthis policy.

INCONSISTENCY IN MEASUREMENT
*Ordinary leakage, ordinary loss in weight or volume, or ordinary wear and tear of the subject-matter insured is excluded.

USED GOODS EXCLUSION
*In no case shall this insurance cover any claims related to second hand goods or commodities in transport with the purpose of repair, maintenance, revision and return.

INSUFFICIENT PACKING
*Loss, damage or expense caused by insufficiency or unsuitability of packing or preparation of the subject matter insured is excluded.

LEGAL REPORTS AND DOCUMENTS NOTE
*The Insured are obliged to notify the Underwriter the occurrence of damage, and take all and any measures to prevent the damage from increasing, as soon as they are informed thereof. The Underwriters shall as soon as possible send an expert to assess the damage at site. It is obligatory that the Insured have the loss or damage suffered by the goods recorded in minutes signed by the carriers and their authorized representative by the time of delivery, and/or that the damage be notified by means of a Notary Public to the carriers or their authorized representative within three days as of the assessment of the damage. Otherwise the loss or damages covered by this insurance policy shall not be indemnified. In case of any claim, the insured is obliged to provide each of the documents required by the insurer such as invoice, invoice approved by customs, affreightment, consignment note, photographes, accident

Page: 1/3
This policy consists of 3 pages and does not constitute any provision by its

Düzenleyen Teknik Personel Adı Soyadı   ANK BİRİKİM SİGORTA
Düzenleyen Teknik Personel Sicil No   201201068
MAPFRE GENEL SİGORTA A.Ş. Ticaret Sicil No: 38676

MAPFRE GENEL SIGORTA A.S.
ANKARA BÖLGE
BIRIKIM SIGORTA ARACILIK HIZMETLERI A.S.

Tel: Fax:
E-mail:

Fig 9.2　Marine Insurance Policy

the goods where a number of consigments of similar export goods are intended to be covered. An open policy covers these shipments, as soon as they are made, under the previous arrangement between the insured and the insurance company.

4.Combined Certificate 联合凭证

When the goods are exported to Hong Kong, and some countries in Southeast Asia, the insurance company sometimes adds the coverage and insurance amount on the commercial invoice which is made out by a foreign trade company. This is a certificate which combines the invoice with the insurance policy. It is the simplest insurance certificate in use.

Section Four   Insurance Practice in China
第四节   我国保险实务

在 CFR 和 CIF 的成效条款下,卖方需要负责运输保险,在 FOB 条款下,卖方也经常代为办理保险,国内有多家保险公司可以承保国际海运货物。本节介绍国内货运保险业务的一般流程。

1.To Insure 投保

When the import and export goods are transported from the port of shipment to the destination, the buyer or the seller is required to insure the goods through insurance companies. In handling the insurance, there need to select the appropriate insurance coverage, determine the amount of insurance, pay insurance premiums, and make out the relevant procedures. When insuring the goods, the followings should be paid attention to: the choice of insurance coverage; determination of insurance amount and calculation of the insurance premiums, etc.

2.Insurance Documents 保险单据

Insurance documents are legal papers to testimony the setting up of theinsurance contract. These documents should state the responsibilities and obligations of the insurer and the insured. They are the certificates to show that the insurer promises to insure the goods, and the insured can lodge claims on the insurer once there are damages or losses.

3.Endorsement of the Insurance Policy 保险单背书

Insurance policy is a document which can be transferred by the endorsement. According to customary practice of international insurance industry, after endorsement by the insured person the ownership right of the insured goods would be transferred the assignee with the ownership right of the insured goods. Before or after the endorsement, the insurance company needs not to be notified.

So, the exporter can complete the transfer procedures by signing the word "endorsement" in the insurance policy.

4.Insurance Claims 保险索赔

The insured person or his agent should do the followings when making claims to the insurer:

a. Loss notification and cargo damage inspection;

b. Reserve the right to make claims on the third-party;

c. Take reasonable rescue measures;

d. Get ready of the certificate for claims.

Quiz 课后思考题

1. 国际贸易中,海运货物在海上运输过程中,可能发生哪些风险?
2. 一切险的承保范围和特点是什么?
3. 保险金额和保险费分别是怎样计算的?
4. 请解释下列术语:海上风险、部分损失、一切险、海动保险。
5. 在国内,为海运货物投保有哪些程序?

Chapter Ten　Textiles Inspection
第十章　纺织品检验

在国际贸易中,产品的质量是双方都关心的核心问题。纺织品检验是按照某种检验标准对纺织品进行的物理性能或化学性能的检测。由于纺织产业链长,产品种类多,因此纺织品是一个很大的检测类别,涉及检验机构、检验标准、检验证书等环节,纺织品外贸跟单员深入了解这些知识可以把控订单质量,减少质量纠纷,使跟单工作顺利开展。

China textile industry and textiles trade will be further integrated into the global economy with the entrance into WTO and more foreign traders will take advantage of our country's rich resources of textile raw material and lower labor costs to participate in the import and export international trade of textiles by means of cooperation, joint stock, exclusive investment and transit trade. Meanwhile, with the increasing of the quality consciousness and demands of consumers at home and abroad and the frequent occurrence of quality disputes in textiles trade, these foreign traders entrust famous international inspection organizations with the inspection service of the qualities of goods in order to protect their own interests. With our country becoming the biggest country of textiles production, export and consumption in the world and the rapid development of the service industry of modern logistics, the service demands of the inspection market will further increase; quite a lot of foreign inspection organizations are trying to make use of the opportunities of opening service market and entering Chinese textiles inspection market to develop the existing inspection market in different ways, thereby occupying a lot of the market.

This chapter mainly introduces commodity inspection clauses and types of inspection certificates, the main inspection agencies at home and abroad and their respective inspection standards and items as well as the inspection and labelling of green textiles or ecological textiles. The introduction makes it quite clear that formation of commodity inspection clauses, legal restriction and economic functions of inspection certificate as well as the meaning, main contents and testing items of green textiles or ecological textiles, etc.

Section One　Major Inspection Agencies and Inspection Standards at Home and Abroad
第一节　国内外主要检验机构及检验标准

本节介绍国内外主要纺织品检验机构及检验标准,包括各个机构的简要历史、业务范围、报告内容等。

The inspection agencies inside our country include the country's official inspection agencies, a lot of non-government inspection agencies, private inspection agencies, semiofficial inspection agencies, some well-known foreign multinational corporations and joint venture inspection agencies. They take part in the inspection of our country's import-export commodities. Some inspection agencies have agreement and keep partnership with many countries in the world, which make contributions to the inspection of our country's import-export commodities. The main inspection agencies and inspection standards of textiles are as the followings.

1. Entry-exit Inspection and Quarantine Bureau of the People's Republic of China 中华人民共和国出入境检验检疫局

In August 1999, the State Council authorized re-establishing the local entry-exit inspection and quarantine agencies all over China and set up the state administration for entry-exit inspection and quarantine by integrating the entry-exit sanitary quarantine under the Ministry of Public Health, the quarantine of animals and plants under the Ministry of Agriculture and the inspection of import-export commodities under the National Bureau of Inspection on Import-Export Commodities, directly under which there are 35 provincial and municipal bureaus responsible for the entry-exit inspection and quarantine, certification and supervising in their respective jurisdictional regions.

(1) Inspecfion standards of textiles

The main reference inspection standards and methods of textiles are as the followings: GB, AATCC (American Association of Textile Chemists Colorists), ASTM (American Society for Testing and Materials), JSA (Japanese Standards Association), ISO (International Organization for Standardization), DIN (Deutsches Institut Fur Normung), BS (British Standards Institution), IWS (International Wool Secretariat), AS (Standard Australia), CAN/CGBS (Canadian General Standards Board), NF (Association Francaise De Normalization), US CPSC (The US Consumer Product Safety Commission), FIMS (The United States Government), SATRA (Shoe and Allied Trades Research Association).

(2) Main inspection items

a. Fiber content. Include wool/cashmere, cotton/viscose, hemp /cotton, the rest.

b. Dimensional change. Include washing, dry cleaning.

c. Color fastness. Include washing, dry cleaning, rubbing / crocking water, light, perspiration, ironing.

d. Physical properties. Include tensile strength, abrasion resistance, bursting strength, tearing strength, seam strength, seam slippage, pilling resistance, yarn counts, pH value, flammability, hydrostatic pressure/spray, fabric weight, warp/weft density, antistatic electricity, care label recommendations.

e. Poisonous and harmful substances. Include banned azo-dyes, formaldehyde, extractable heavy-metals, pesticide, preservative.

2. Textiles Testing Office，Testing Technique Center on Industrial Raw Material，Shanghai Entry-exit Inspection and Quarantine Bureau 上海出入境检验检疫局工业原材料检测技术中心纺织品检测室

It mainly deals with the testing of textiles including clothes，industrial textiles，other textile replica and ecological textiles，and the scientific research of textiles testing. It passed the certification by the former commodity inspection system first-class lab in 1989 and passed the re-checking by the former State Administration for Import and Export Commodity Inspection and gained the accreditation certificate in December，1995. It won the accreditation of China National Accreditation Board for Laboratories (CNAL) in 2002 and was accredited by China Certification Committee for Environmental Labelling Produce (CCCEL) in 2001 and was appointed as the testing lab of ecological textiles. In 1909，it was appointed as testing center of pure wool mark by International Wool Secretariat (IWS).

Textiles testing office，testing technology center on industrial raw material，Shanghai Entry-Exit Inspection and Quarantine Bureau offers the following inspection and test description of textiles and clothes (Fig 10.1) .

Test Category	Test Items			
(1) Test Description of Color Fastness	Washing Rubbing/crocking (dry & wet) Water Perspiration Hot pressing	Dry cleaning Light Organic solvents Sea water Chlorinated pool water	Light and perspiration Bleaching	
(2) Analysis and Test Description of Fabric Texture Fabric width	Fabric thickness Fabric weight per unit area Fabric count of woven fabric Yarn counts of woven fabric			
(3) Test Description of Quality	Tensile strength Tearing strength Bursting strength Seam breaking strength Seam slippage	Abrasion resistance Pilling resistance Water repellency Static water pressure Washing shrinkage	Dry cleaning Flammability Air permeability UV transmittance Development of care label	Measurement of color differences Electrostatic performance test
(4) Fiber Analysis and Other Analysis and Test Description	Qualitative analysis Quantitative analysis			
(5) Test and Inspection Description of Fiber and Tan	Fiber diameter Melting point of fibers Yarncount Yarnt wist Regain of yarn	Single thread strength Yarn evenness		
(6) IWS Pure Wool Mark Test Description	Fabric strength Light fastness Fastness to water Fabric weight Fiber diameter	Dry burst strength Dimensional stability Abrasion Seam slippage DCM extract	ICI pilling Fiber content Fastness to rubbing Cover factor of knitted Alkali perspiration	Stretch and growth Fastness to severe washing Martindale pilling Fastness to hand washing Spirality of knitwear
(7) Test Description of Ecological Textiles	pH value Formaldehyde content Azo dyestuffs Determination of heavy metals PCP content	Pesticide Determination of odor Colorfastness to water Colorfastness to rubbing Colorfastness to perspiration	Colorfastness to saliva	

Fig 10.1   Test Categories and Test Items

3. Quality Supervision and Inspection Center of National Cotton Textiles 国家棉纺织产品质量监督检验中心

The Center is the initial national quality inspection center attached to China Textile Academy. The center can do a comprehensive inspection on all kinds of fiber，yarn and three main kinds of textiles for clothes, ornament and industry according to the standards of ISO, IWS, ASTM, AATCC, JIS, BS and GB. Every year, the center takes on the inspection entrusted by textile enterprises, scientific research institutes, schools, circulation fields, arbitration organizations and common consumers from all over the country. The all-round service of the center includes:

a. The supervision and inspection, quality evaluation authorized by the national management departments.

b. The performance test and analysis of textile material and textiles as well as the quality determination and arbitration.

c. Regular inspection, supervision of inspection and production of the entrusted products qualities.

d. Offer assuring quality service such as ordering agreement, shipments supervision and inspection on arrival goods, etc.

e. Research, service, consultation and training of testing technology. The main inspection and testing categories and projects can be found in the chart 15 from page 540 to 543 in the reference book "*The Technical Regulations for Textiles and International Trade*" published by China Textile & Apparel Press.

4.SGS-CSTC Standard Technical Service Ltd, Shanghai Branch 上海通用标准技术服务有限公司

SGS – CSTC is a joint venture co-established by SGS and China Standard Technology Development Corp. attached to the former Sate Bureau of Quality and Technical Supervision in 1991. The company in succession sets up 15 branch offices in Beijing, Shanghai, Tianjin, Dalian, Qingdao, Guangzhou, Xiamen, Shenzhen, Ningbo, Qinhuangdao, Nanjing, Zhanjiang, Wuhan, etc. with its service covering inspection, testing and certification. In addition, the 10 professional labs are established including textiles lab, cashmere fiber lab and so on.

The textiles testing service offered by SGS-CSTC includes regulative testing, functional testing, green environment protection testing, safety performance testing, etc. The involved products include fiber, yarn, carpet, accessories of ready-made clothes, feather, eider products, gloves and leather products. The standards adopted cover the standards of ISO, AATCC, ASTM, EN, CAN/CGSB, DIN, BS, AS, JIS, etc. Fig 10.2 shows the test results for a non-woven fabric of face mask.

The main testing projects and the corresponding testing standards offered by the company can be found from page 515 to 522 in the reference book *The Technical Regulations for Textiles and International Trade* published by China Textile & Apparel Press.

5. Japan Synthetic Textile Inspection Institute Foundation Shanghai Kakon Apparel Test & Mending Co., Ltd.日本化学纤维检查协会上海科恳服装检验修整有限公司

Shanghai Kakon Apparel Test & Mending Co., Ltd. is a joint venture company of Corporate Body

SGS

Test Report   No. SHAHG1711802301   Date: 13 Jun 2017   Page 1 of 3

XINYUAN INTERNATIONAL DEVELOPMENT CO.,LTD

ROOM 2103 & 2016,BLUE WHALE MANSION,SHENGLI RD,HEFEI P.C.230011,CHINA

The following sample(s) was/were submitted and identified on behalf of the clients as : NONWOVEN FACE MASK

SGS Job No. :   SHHL17060297750T - SH

Date of Sample Received :   07 Jun 2017

Testing Period :   07 Jun 2017 - 13 Jun 2017

Test Requested :   Selected test(s) as requested by client.

Test Method :   Please refer to next page(s).

Test Results :   Please refer to next page(s).

Result Summary :

Test Requested	Conclusion
RoHS Directive 2011/65/EU	See Results

Signed for and on behalf of
SGS-CSTC Standards Technical Services (Shanghai) Co., Ltd.

Serena Wang
Approved Signatory

Fig 10.2   SGS Test Results Sample

Japan Synthetic Textile Inspection Institute Foundation and Hongxin Industrial CO., Ltd. in Shanghai Hongqiao development zone. With the development of the trade of textiles exported to Japan, Japan Synthetic Textile Inspection Institute Foundation in succession has set up testing centers in Shanghai, Qingdao, Ningbo and Dalian since 1994.

Shanghai Kakon Apparel Test & Mending Co., Ltd. passed ISO 9001 quality system accreditation in 2001, and has been accredited by China National Accreditation Board forLaboratories (CNAL). As the first accredited textiles test company of Japan−China joint venture, it has developed to be the biggest joint company for the test and mending of textiles exported to Japan in China.

The test items and standards can be found from page 532 to 533 in the reference book *The Technical Regulations for Textiles and International Trade* published by China Textile & Apparel Press.

Section Two　Inspection and Labelling of Green Textiles or Ecological Textiles
第二节　绿色纺织品或生态纺织品的检验与标志

近年来,随着国内外对环保问题的日益重视,绿色纺织品的概念已被越来越多的生产商和消费者接受,很多发达国家将纺织品的"绿色、环保、无害"等要求作为一种技术壁垒,我国也制定了相关法律以规范生产者的行为。纺织行业节能减排,打造绿色纺织已是大势所趋。

1.Meaning and Main Contents of Green Textiles or Ecological Textiles 绿色纺织品或生态纺织品的含义和主要内容

With the occurrence of international hotspot of environmental protection, the public environmental awareness has been raised. Consumers will spontaneously resist environmentally unfriendly products during the process of production and consumption and are more and more concerned with green, nonpoisonous and ecological products. They prefer to choose the products healthful to human body and harmless to environment. As a result, green products and their consumption become the leading trend in international trade.

Green textile means the use of new−type natural raw material, publicly harmless dyestuff and technology as well as health pure raw material and products, which will be the main part of future textile industry, green textile includes the development of textile resources, the production process of textiles and the technology, the sale and using of textiles and the disposal of waste.

Ecological textiles can also be called green textiles or environmentally harmonious textiles. In recent years, a lot of scientists have dealt with the establishment and research of textile ecology and put forward its theoretical system. Textile ecology can be classified as production ecology, consumption ecology, and disposal ecology.

2.Ecolabelling of Green Textiles 绿色纺织品的生态标志

In order to adapt to the implementation of related laws and regulations and to meet the wave of green consumption, the international commodities producers and managers take the opportunity to promote the environmentally friendly textiles and clothes, the signs or labellings of green environmentally friendly textiles come into being naturally. The textile clothes with environmentally friendly labellings or figures indicate that their quality are not only qualified but also are up to the regulated demands of environmental protection during the process of production, using, consumption and disposal, and suggest that they are harmless to the ecological environment and human body or can reduce all kinds of dangers by taking proper measures. The international frequently used green labellings nowadays are introduced as follows.

(1) Oeko-Tex Standard 100

The labelling, Oeko-Tex Standard 100, is a set of standards to test harmful substances in textiles, which is early set up by Professor Wilhelm Herzog in Austrian Textile Research Institute in Vienna with the aim of indicating that the textiles produced in Austria comply with the strict demands of human consuming ecology. Thus, the first standard concerning textile ecology–Austrian Textile Standard ONT100 was issued. In November 1991, professor Wilhelm Herzog had a first talk with Professor J. Mecheels in Corman Hohenstein Research Institute discussing their cooperation in the field of textiles consumption ecology. They changed ONT100 into Oeko-Tex Standard 100, which is to be used to test the ecological effects of textiles and clothes to human beings. The standard includes the analysis of some harmful parameters and their dosage limits. If the product can accord with the standard, a labelling is issued which indicates that the textile is trustful in accordance to the Oeko-Tex Standard 100 for the testing of harmful substances. Fig 10.3 is a figure of Ecological textiles labelling on clothes products.

Fig 10.3   Oeko-Tex Standard 100 Label

Oeko-Tex Standard 100 generalizes the framework of applying and granting labellings: Oeko-Tex Standard 101–116 define some requirements and limit maximum of parameter: Oeko-Tex Standard 200 introduces the testing method.

(2) Eco-tex

The labeling, Eco-tex, is set up by German Eco-tex Association. The service of the association is to audit and recommend the optimal ecological textiles. The association sets up an ecological testing system for traders and import, and ensures the ecological optimization of the delivered goods between suppliers. The Eco-tex labelling can be awarded to the enterprises that have set up ecological testing system. The standards for Eco-tex ecological testing system include the following aspects.

a. Provide the documents of the whole textiles production process from fiber, spinning, weaving, dyeing and printing to garment.

b. All the chemical substances used during the process of production should be safe, such as dyes and aids, and there should be documents that can prove their safety.

c. Without the using of chlorinated organic bleaching agent.

d. No kerosene is used in printing system.

e. The using of banned and toxic dyes is not allowed.

f. The working place that is acceptable in the society.

g. The ecologically harmful substances are reduced in the production.

(3) Arbeitskreis Naturtexilien

The labeling, Arbeitskreis Naturtexilien, is an ecolabelling which is strictly demanded based on final products. It is made by four kinds of natural textiles work groups which are composed of 20 member companies. They define natural textiles as the clothes or textiles which are produced by natural fiber of plant or animal and are not treated, treated or dyed by nontoxic dyes. Accessories or chemical reagent used for treatment can not contain ethoxylated compound, formaldehyde, glyoxal, heavy metals, substances that can form organic halogen, etc.

(4) Comitextil

Facing the increasing of Ecolabellings, European Economic Community (EEC) Textile Industry Committee set up a labelling Comitextil aimed at final goods in order to provide European associations with ecolabellings of products. The labelling is similar to Clean Fashion and Steilmann which is only suitable to some products within the range of company. The qualities of the delivered goods must meet the standard, and at the same time, the standard limit must be written into the delivery agreement. Comitextil is an internal labelling, which is mainly used to distinguish whether a product can meet the ecological demands.

(5) Clean Fashion

The labeling, Clean Fashion, is set up based on final products, which is made by the biggest textile sellers in the world. Its regulation about formaldehyde content assembles the criterions of MST, OTNIOO, Comitextil and Eco Mark. Its regulation about pesticide assembles the standard of MST, Steilmann and Eco Mark. Its regulation about colorants and heavy metals is similar to other ecolabellings. But there is no regulation about hypochlorite bleaching and halogen carrier.

(6) Eco Mark

The labeling, Eco Mark, is set up by Indian Ministry of Environment and Forest in cooperation with Indian Standard Bureau for environmentally friendly products, with its criterions conforming to international standards.

(7) North European Environment Labelling

North European Environment Labelling, put forward by SIS, is an ecolabelling used for producing natural fiber under the organic conditions without agrochemical and synthetic fertilizer.

3.Testing Items of Ecological Textiles 生态纺织品的检验项目

At present, it is a common phenomenon that the buyers of textiles and clothes in the main countries in Europe and America highlight the consumption of green textile ready-made clothes. They have more strict demands on the process of production of textile clothes and its final products. To meet the demands, all kinds of the third inspection organizations at home and abroad offer a lot of new inspection and testing items to adapt to the internal and external environmental protection and safety performance demands of the green textiles or ecological textiles. Generally, all kinds of main testing items of Eco Textile are as follows: pH Value, formaldehyde, heavy metals residues, PCP content, azo colorants, colorfastness to rubbing, fastness to water, allergic dye, colorfastness to perspiration, colorfastness to saliva (for baby wear only), inflammability finish, pesticides residues, PCB content, chlorinated organic compounds, release of nickel, ozone depleting chemicals.

Section Three　Commodity Inspection Clauses and Inspection Certificates
第三节　商检条款及商检证书

纺织品的检验条款以及检验证书在很多合同或信用证中有相应的规定,纺织品外贸跟单员经常需要处理此类问题。本节主要介绍了商检条款、出境货物报检单和一些有代表性的商检证书。

1.Commodity Inspection Clauses 商检条款

(1) Formation of commodity inspection clauses

Commodity inspection clauses are one of the important clauses in an international trade sales contract. Commodity inspection clauses in the contract can be classified into two kinds: the quality and quantity clauses and inspection and claim clauses.

a. Quality and quantity clauses. These clauses are the specific clauses about the export-import commodities' quality, specification, grade, packing, quantity, weight, etc. Different commodities and contracts have different clauses. Quality and quantity clauses are an important standard to judge whether export-import commodities are qualified. The contents of the clauses must be specific and clear; its use of language and data must be precise, appropriate and convenient for inspection and clarification of responsibilities. The vague expressions such as "about" "or so" "advanced equipment" "fare quality" must be avoided.

b. Inspection and claim clauses. Inspection and claim clauses are the clauses about inspection and delivery as well as re-inspection and claim, including inspection of shipper, inspection organizations, time and place of inspection, reinspection of consignee, reinspection organizations, deadline of claim, JSPCC fees, inspection certificates, arbitration, etc.

(2)Time and place of inspection

There are no unified legal regulations about theways of inspection of export-import commodities in the world. Usually, the time and place of inspection should be stipulated in a sales contract by both the buyers and sellers. There are three ways to stipulate the time and place of inspection in international trade.

①There are two methods of inspection in a country of export.

a. Inspection at the place of origin. It is the seller who entrust the inspection organization with the inspection.

b. Inspection at the port of shipment before or at the time of shipment. The quality of the offshore goods is regarded as the inspection norm, which is made by the inspection organization agreed by the two parties, and in this case the certificate available from the inspection agency at the port of shipment is one of the documents about the goods' quality.

②There are two methods of inspection in a country of import.

a. Inspection at the port of destination after unloading. The quality of the landed goods is regarded as the inspection norm and the certificate available from the inspection agency at the port of destination is a basis as claim. Should the quality be found not in conformity with that of the contract, the seller should take responsibility for it.

b. Inspection at the buyer's office or the place of the final users. This method is suitable for the inspection of those products which need installation and adjustment, such as serial equipments, machines, electrons and instruments, etc.

③Inspection in a country of export and re-inspection in a country of import.

The inspection certificate at the port/place of shipment is one of the documents for payment and the buyer has the right to re-inspect. This method is convenient and fair for both sides, which is often adopted nowadays. Here is an example of inspection and claim clauses.

It is mutually agreed that the Certificate of Quality andWeight (Quantity) issued by China Entry-Exit Inspection and Quarantine Bureau at the port/place of shipment shall be part of the documents to be presented for negotiation under the relevant L/C. The Buyers shall have the right to re-inspect the quality and weight (quantity) of the cargo. The re-inspection fee shall be borne by the buyers. Should the quality and/or weight (quantity) be found not in conformity with that of the contract, the buyers are entitled to lodge with the sellers a claim which should be supported by survey reports issued by a recognized surveyor approved by the sellers. The claim, if any, shall be lodged within⋯ days after arrival of the cargo at the port/place of destination.

2.Declaration Form on Export Commodity 出境货物报检单

According to regulations of Law of the People's Republic of China on Import and Export Commodity Inspection, declaration form on export commodity is an application form of export commodities applied to the designated commodity inspection authorities for inspection, which includes description of goods, specification, quantity / weight, packing place of origin, etc. Fig 10.4 is a sample of declaration form om export commodity.

出境货物报检单

报检单位 (加盖公章)：艾格进出口贸易公司					* 编　号 EC0001876	

报检单位登记号：3200000986　联系人　张艾格　　　电话：86-21-23501213　　　报检日期：2017 年 08 月 30 日

发货人	（中文）	艾格进出口贸易公司					
	（外文）	AIGE IMPORT & EXPORT COMPANY					
收货人	（中文）	日清进出口贸易公司					
	（外文）	RIQING EXPORT AND IMPORT COMPANY					

货物名称（中/外文）	H.S.编码	产地	数/重量	货物总值	包装种类及数量
男式T恤衫 MEN'S T-SHIRT	6109100010	中国	2000 件	USD 30000	100 纸箱

运输工具名称号码	TBA		贸易方式	一般贸易	货物存放地点	SHANGHAI CY
合同号	CONTRACT02		信用证号		用途	
发货日期	2017-08-30	输往国家(地区)	日本	许可证 / 审批号		
启运地	上海	到达口岸	名古屋	生产单位注册号		
集装箱规格、数量及号码	LCL					

合同、信用证订立的检验 检疫条款或特殊要求	标记及号码	随附单据（划"√"或补填）	
	MEN'S T-SHIRT JAPAN C/NO.1-100 MADE IN CHINA	☑合同 □信用证 ☑发票 □换证凭单 ☑装箱单 □厂检单	□包装性能结果单 □许可/审批文件 □ □ □ □

需要证单名称（划"√"或补填）				*检验检疫费
☑品质证书	1 正 3 副	☑植物检疫证书	1正 3 副	总金额（人民币元）
☑重量证书	1 正 3 副	□熏蒸/消毒证书	正 副	
☑数量证书	1 正 3 副	□出境货物换证凭证		
□兽医卫生证书	正 副	☑通关单		计费人
☑健康证书	1 正 3 副			
□卫生证书	正 副			收费人
□动物卫生证书	正 副			

报检人郑重声明： 　1.本人被授权报检。 　2.上列填写内容正确属实，货物无伪造或冒用他人的厂名、标志、认证标志，并承担货物质量责任。 　　　　　　　签名：　张艾格		领取证单	
		日期	
		签名	

注：有"＊"号栏由出入境检验检疫机关填写

◆国家出入境检验检疫局制

[1-2 (2000.1.1)]

Fig 10.4　出境货物报检单

3.Inspection Certificates 商检证书

（1）Legal restrictions and economic functions of Inspection Certificates

The documents of handing-over and settlement can be used for dealing with claim under the symbolic delivery system in most modern foreign trade. The relevant national laws, regulations, foreign trade contracts and international trade convention grant the just legal restrictions to all kinds of inspection certificates and surveyor's report issued by official inspection organizations and independent inspection and certification organizations.

The quality, weight, quantity and damage approved by commodity inspection certificates are the certification result and assessment, which is directly associated with the responsibilities and economic rights and interests (including the ownership and limitation of responsibilities) of both the buyers and sellers, transport company, insurance company, etc.in foreign trade . As a result, commodity inspection certificates are certifications with economic force that the relevant all sides care about. From the economic angle, commodity inspection certificates have the following functions.

a. The quality, weight and quantity certificates of import and export commodities are the warrant of negotiation.

b. Commodity inspection certificates are effective warrants of counting freight.

c. Commodity inspection certificates are effective warrants of making a claim.

d. Commodity inspection certificates are effective warrant of counting the tariff.

e. They can be used as an effective warrant of customs declaration, inspection and permit.

f. They can be used as an effective warrant of implementing a contract or not.

g. They can be used as an effective warrant of handing-over and settlement.

h. They can be used as an effective warrant of illustration of arbitration and litigation.

(2) Types of Commodity Inspection Certificates

There are many types of commodity inspection certificates. The certificates concerning textile fiber and its products mainly include the following.

a. Quality certificate (certificate of quality). It is a certificate verifying the quality and specification of the goods. Quality certificate can be used to verify whether import-export commodities conform to the sale contract and the other stipulations. It is an effective warrant for acceptance of goods, clearing payment, external claim, settlement of claims, customs clearance, inspection and permit, arbitration and litigation.

b. Weight certificate or quantity certificate. It is a certificate verifying the weight or quantity of the goods. Weight certificate or quantity certificate proves whether the weight or qualities of import-export commodities accord with the stipulations in the international trade contract and is an effective warrant for the settlement and issuing of bill of lading of the exported goods, the clearing payment and external claim of the imported goods. Weight certificate is also an effective credential for customs declaration, taxation, counting freight and handling costs. Fig 10.5 shows a form for weight certificate.

c. Certificates of origin. It is a credential for the export commodities in the import country to go through customs formalities, enjoy the preferential treatment of the reduction of tariff and prove the place of origin of the commodities. Certificates of origin include Certificate of Origin, generalized System of Preferences Certificate of Origin Form A(GSP), Certificate of Origin for Textile Products, etc.

The Certificate of Origin of the People's Republic of China can be called Certificate of Origin

中华人民共和国出入境检验检疫
**ENTRY-EXIT INSPECTION AND QUARANTINE
OF THE PEOPLE'S REPUBLIC OF CHINA**

正 本
ORIGINAL

重 量 证 书
WEIGHT CERTIFICATE

编号 No.: 370021206260142

发货人 Consignor	ZHENGZHOU DADE GROUP CO.,LTD 3032,HUAKAI BUILDING,21# JINGQI ROAD,ZHENGZHOU,CHINA
收货人 Consignee	RURAL TECHNOLOGY DEVELOPMENT JOINT STOCK COMPANY LAC HONG, VAN LAM, HUNG YEN, VIETNAM TEL/FAX: 84 4 4455.1368/1369
品名 Description of Goods	SOYBEAN MEAL-FEED GRADE
报检数量 / 重量 Quantity / Weight Declared	300000KGS
包装种类及数量 Number and Type of Packages	6000PLASTIC BAGS
运输工具 Means of Conveyance	BY SEA, BALTIC STRAIT

标记及号码
Mark & No.

GROSS WEIGHT: 300.000MT
NET WEIGHT: 300.660MT

附加声明 ADDITIONAL DECLARATION

序号 CONTAINER NO.	集装箱号 CONTAINER NO.	铅封号 SEAL NO.	毛重 GROSS WEIGHT (kg)	净重 NTE WEIGHT (kg)	件数 NO.OF BAGS	体积 MEASUREMENT (CBM)
1	DFSU2105257	TSY0208270	20044.00	20000.00	400	25
2	FCIU2362919	TSY0208992	20044.00	20000.00	400	25
3	FCIU2372959	TSY0208911	20044.00	20000.00	400	25
4	TGHU0903586	TSY0208964	20044.00	20000.00	400	25
5	FCIU2365190	TSY0208933	20044.00	20000.00	400	25
6	DFSU2791286	TSY0208931	20044.00	20000.00	400	25
7	TSLU0202037	TSY0208987	20044.00	20000.00	400	25
8	TGHU0923330	TSY0203985	20044.00	20000.00	400	25
9	FCIU3914015	TSY0203972	20044.00	20000.00	400	25
10	TCKU3597400	TSY0203959	20044.00	20000.00	400	25
11	TCKU3817166	TSY0203998	20044.00	20000.00	400	25
12	TCKU2647830	TSY0203995	20044.00	20000.00	400	25
13	TCKU2474484	TSY0203946	20044.00	20000.00	400	25
14	TSLU0225599	TSY0215599	20044.00	20000.00	400	25
15	TGHU0849422	TSY0215590	20044.00	20000.00	400	25
		TOTALS:	300660.00	300000.00	6000	375

Issued by Independent Surveyor

*** *** ***

签证地点 Place of Issue QINGDAO, CHINA 签证日期 Date of Issue 16.OCT.2012

Official Stamp 授权签字人 Authorized Officer LI WEN 签 名 Signature

我们以上所列数据是最大程度上的实核。本证书不解除买方和其他有关方面合同和法定之事。本证书亦不免除卖方其他责任。All inspection are carried out conscientiously to the best of our knowledge and ability. This certificate does not in any respect absolve the seller and other related parties from his contractual and legal obligations especially when product quality is concerned.

[e e-4(2000.1.1)]

AA0434856

Fig 10.5 Weight Certificate

shortly, which is a document to certify the place in which the export goods are produced and is in conformity with Rules of the People's Republic of China on the Origin of Export Goods. Certificate of Origin can be issued or certified by the embassies and consulates in the import country or by the official certification agency or chamber of commerce in the export county.

Generalized System of Preferences Certificate of Origin Form A can be also called Certificate of Origin for GSP or GSP Form A. Generalized system of preferences is a preferential tariff system granted by developed countries to the commodities, especially the semi-finished products and finished products from the developing countries, whose principle is universal, non-discriminatory and non-reciprocal. The preference-receiving country should provide the GSP Form A of the commodities under GSP for the preference-giving country. Certificate of Origin for Textile Products is suitable for the textiles and issued by CIQ. Fig 10.6 is a sample Form A for women's blouse.

ORIGINAL   4713448911

1. Goods consigned from (Exporter's business name, address, country)	Reference No. G144702C45300004
SHENZHEN JIN TONGCAN TRADE CO., LTD	GENERALIZED SYSTEM OF PREFERENCES
B10D REITH INTERNATIONAL BUILDING XINXIU ROAD	CERTIFICATE OF ORIGIN
LUOHU SHENZHEN CHINA	(Combined declaration and certificate)
	FORM A
2. Goods consigned to (Consignee's name, address, country)	Issued in THE PEOPLE'S REPUBLIC OF CHINA
PEEK & CLOPPENBURG KG	(country)
BERLINER ALLEE 2	
D-40212 DUSSELDORF	See Notes overleaf
GERMANY	
3. Means of transport and route (as far as known)	4. For official use
FROM DALIAN CHINA TO GERMANY BY SEA	

5. Item number	6. Marks and numbers of packages	7. Number and kind of packages; description of goods	8. Origin criterion (see Notes overleaf) "P"	9. Gross weight or other quantity	10. Number and date of invoices
1	N/M	CTNS OF LADIES' 90% POLYESTER 10% ELASTANE WOVEN BLOUSE ORDER NO: 3408678/3408679/3408680/3408681/3432659 ARTICLE NO: 14S2J103 PACKING IN CTNS TOTAL: SEVENTY SEVEN (77) CTNS ONLY *** *** *** *** *** ***		542PCS	JDD-TP&C1305 JAN. 02, 2014

11. Certification	12. Declaration by the exporter
It is hereby certified... control carried out, that the declaration by the exporter is correct.	The undersigned hereby declares that the above details and statements are correct; that all the goods were produced in
	0000039388950
	and that they comply with the origin requirements specified for those goods in the Generalized System of Preferences for goods exported to
	GERMANY

Fig 10.6   Sample Certificate of Origin Form A

Quiz　课后思考题

1. 中华人民共和国出入境检验检疫局对于纺织品的主要检验项目有哪些？
2. 什么叫绿色纺织品？它对人们的消费行为产生怎样的影响？
3. 简述 Oeko-Tex Standard 100 的特点？
4. 查阅资料，列举 Form A 产地证的主要内容。

参考文献

［1］邵作仁.外贸跟单操作实务［M］.北京：中国商务出版社，2016.

［2］刘昭林，王金泉.实用纺织服装出口操作指南［M］.北京：中国纺织出版社，2012.

［3］托托拉，默克尔，黄故.仙童英汉双解纺织词典［M］.北京：中国纺织出版社，2004.

［4］檀文茹.国际贸易专业英语［M］.3 版.北京：对外经贸大学出版社，2014.

［5］黄故. 纺织英语［M］.北京：中国纺织出版社，2008.

［6］KAVI Kumar K S. A Study of India's Textile Exports and Environmental Regulations［M］. Gateway East：Springer Nature Singapore Pte Ltd，2018.

Appendix 附录

1.Terminology Practice 术语解析

（1）关于质量跟单的常见术语及解释

① **Spread**：The price difference between two related markets or commodities. For example，the April-August live cattle spread.

② **Speculator**：A market participant who tries to profit from buying and selling futures and option contracts by anticipating future price movements. Speculators assume market price risk and add liquidity and capital to the futures markets. They do not hold equal and opposite cash market risks.

③ **Option**：A contract that conveys the right，but not the obligation，to buy or sell a futures contract at a certain price for a specified time period. Only the seller（writer）of the option is obligated to perform.

④ **Maintenance margin**：A set minimum margin（per outstanding futures contract）that a customer must maintain in a margin account.

⑤ **Cash（spot）market**：A place where people buy and sell the actual（cash）commodities，that is，a grain elevator，livestock market，or the like.

⑥ **Adding value**：Adding something that the customer wants was not there before.

⑦ **Benchmarking**：Comparing your product to the best competitors.

⑧ **Bring to the table**：Refers to what each individual in a meeting can contribute to a meeting for example，a design or brainstorming meetings.

⑨ **Concurrent（or simultaneous）engineering**：Integrating the design，manufacturing，and test processes.

⑩ **Continuous improvement**：The PDSA（Plan-Do-Study-Act）process of iteration which results in improving a product.

⑪ **Customer satisfaction**：Meeting or exceeding a customer's expectations for a product or service.

⑫ **Design**：The creation of a specification from concepts.

⑬ **Flow charting**：Creating a "map" of the steps in a process.

⑭ **Manufacturing**：Creating a product from specifications.

⑮ **Metrics**：Ways to measure：eg. time，cost，customer satisfaction，quality.

⑯ **Process**：What is actually done to create a product.

⑰ **Six-sigma quality**：Meaning 99.999 997% perfect；only 3.4 defects in a million.

⑱ **Statistical process control（SPC）**：used for measuring the conformance of a product to specifications.

⑲ **Test**：A procedure for critical evaluation，a means of determining the presence，quality，or truth of something, eg.testing the product for defects.

（2）关于数量跟单的常见术语及解释

① **Tare Weight**：The weight of a container and/or packing materials without the weight of the goods it contains.

② **Shipping weight**：Shipping weight represents the gross weight in kilograms of shipments, including the weight of moisture content, wrappings, crates, boxes and containers (other than cargo vans and similar substantial outer containers).

③ **Related parties**：

Members of the same family, spouse, and lineal descendants.

Officers or directors if each individual is also an officer or director of the other organization.

Partners.

Person owning, controlling or holding with power to vote 5% or more of outstanding stock.

Person who is an officer or director in both organizations.

④ **Movement certificate**：Required where goods are being exported from the EU to a country covered by EU trade agreements. These certificates ensure preferential rates of duty on an exporter's goods.

⑤ **Open General Import Licence (OGIL)**：Available from the Department of Trade and Industry, this allows the import of most goods from outside the European Union (EU) without licensing formalities. But some goods require a special licence and are listed in a schedule to OGIL.

⑥ **Pre-shipment Inspection (PSD)**：A few countries require goods and documents to be examined before export by an independent agency. In some countries it's optional but can be requested by the customer. Usually, countries where PSI applies have appointed one dedicated agency to perform the pre-shipment inspection. Normally, your freight forwarder or customer will be able to advise on the necessary arrangements.

⑦ **Payment in advance**：An exporter may be able to negotiate these terms for all or part of its shipment. The exporter bears no risks or financing costs. Payment or part-payment in advance is typically used for low-value sales to individuals or new customers.

⑧ **Quota**：Quantity of a particular type of goods that a country allows to be imported before levying duty or restrictions.

⑨ **Reduced rates of duty**：Some goods can be imported into the UK at a nil or reduced rate of customs duty because they originated in a preference country or are from a non-EU country and qualify for a temporary suspension of customs duty.

⑩ **Terms of delivery**：Cover the division of responsibility for the costs of an export or import sale and for the risk of loss or damage in transit.

⑪ **Tariff quotas**：EU system to allow the importation of limited amounts of certain goods (sometimes from specified countries) at a rate of duly lower than would otherwise apply.

（3）关于包装跟单的常见术语及解释

① **Acquisition**：The process through which resources are obtained to meet determined requirements, methods include purchase, rent, lease, or borrow.

② **Certificate of packing and unpacking** : The document showing the amount of packing and unpacking performed by the agent.

③ **Container (carton)** : A sturdily constructed box used in packing.

④ **Equipment** : Any item with a unit price of US$500 or more (including freight and installation) that does not lose its identity by incorporation into a larger unit and has an expected life of over two years.

⑤ **Hospitality** : A room used for entertaining, i.e., cocktail party, etc. Usually a function room or parlor.

⑥ **Gas packing** : Packaging in a gas-tight container in which any air has been replaced by a gas that contains practically no free oxygen, such as commercial carbon dioxide or nitrogen.

⑦ **Grading** : The selection of produce for certain purposes. Produce is sorted for size, color, quality, ripeness, etc. May be done manually or mechanically on sizing belts.

⑧ **Cubic Feet** (*CF*) : Volume of a shipment using the most extreme dimensions in inches. The formula is : length (in) $\times$ width (in) $\times$ height (in) $/1728 = CF$.

⑨ **Certified lumber** : Lumber that has been treated for parasites either through heat or chemicals, and then inspected to meet certification requirements. Non-coniferous (hardwood) and manufactured (plywood) generally do not need to be certified.

⑩ **Class** : All items that are shipped are divided into various classifications that play a part in determining the cost to ship them. Different "Class" examples are electronics, machineries, and household goods. Each Class is assigned its own number (See "NMFC Number and Class").

⑪ **Crate** : Wooden box built around the product being shipped, provides the best protection for items being shipped.

⑫ **Declared value** : Amount the shipper values any item or shipment. Not a declaration of insurance value. As with release value, insurance must be arranged for in advance of the shipment.

⑬ **Dimensional Weight (DW)** : Typically used for "air" or "international" shipments. Dimensional Weight is also considered "Billable Weight" (minimum charge) regardless of actual weight, if less than DW. The formula is : length (in) $\times$ width (in) $\times$ height (in) $/194 = dw$.

⑭ **Fulfillment** : The act of storing product, filling orders, and shipping for an outside company.

⑮ **Full Truck Load (FTL)** : Any shipment that takes up more than 1/2 trailer full, or the trailer is used for one shipment no matter how much room is used.

⑯ **Inside delivery** : The carrier will deliver product just inside the first room encountered through the closest ground-floor door to the street.

⑰ **Less Than Load (LTL)** : Any shipment that is less than 1/2 trailer full, and can be with other shipments.

⑱ **Lift-gate service** : Hydraulic platform on the rear of the trailer or truck that lifts items up or down. Typically used when item is very heavy (more weight than one person can handle safely) and there is no forklift or dock available to unload. Lift gate services often incur additional charges.

⑲ **National Motor Freight Classification （NMFC）**：Rules, regulations, and classification pertaining to freight moved by a motor carrier.

⑳ **NMFC Number and Class**：Classification numbers assigned to an item dealing mostly with density. The class determines the level of pricing for an item.

㉑ Pallet：A flat wooden structure used to collect items to be shipped on. Allows a forklift or pallet jack to safely move the product around.

㉒ **Pro－number**：Number assigned to a shipment for tracking purpose.

㉓ **Pup**：a freight trailer that is 28 feet long.

㉔ **Reefer**：Nickname for a refrigerated freight trailer. Has nothing to do with any controlled substance.

㉕ **Release value**：Not considered a declaration of insurance value. Typically spoken of in terms of value per pound. Based on classing rules governed by the NMFC. If damage were to happen, a claim can be filed on a customer's behalf up to the release value, but a settlement is not guaranteed.

㉖ **Residential delivery**：Delivery in a residential area, including businesses run from home. This service is to the sidewalk or driveway only. Also known as curbside delivery. Residential deliveries will incur an additional charge. Also, the consignee must have the means to handle the item after it is removed from the truck.

㉗ **Stretch film**：A protective barrier used to hold a collection of goods together, and to keep dust and precipitation off of product. In some cases, a black stretch film is used for UV protection and security.

（4）关于运输跟单的常见术语及解释

① Shipping documents：Documents such as commercial invoices, bills of lading, policies insurance, etc., involved in the shipping of goods.

② **Commercial invoice**：A document prepared by a seller giving details of goods supplied, their contract terms and the total amount due to be paid by the buyer.

③ **Bill of Lading(B/L)**：A document signed by a ship's master, acknowledging receipt of cargo. It also serves as a contract of freight, and as title to the cargo.

④ **Consignment**：A parcel of goods sent by one party to another.

⑤ **Consignee**：the person, firm, or representative to whom a seller of shipper sends merchandise who, upon presentation of the necessary documents, is recognized as the owner of the merchandise.

⑥ **Short weight**：A consignee makes a claim for short weight against the supplier when he finds that the quantity of goods on arrival is less than that shown in the invoice and other documents.

⑦ **Transshipment**：Transferring a cargo from one carrying vessel to another at an immediate port. Before arrival at the ultimate port of destination.

⑧ **Title**：a legal right to the ownership of goods or property.

⑨ **On board B/L**：An on－board Bill of Lading certifies that a consignment has actually been loaded on the carrying vessel; opposed to an alongside Bill of Lading.

⑩ **Alongside**：A term applied to, e. g. a Bill of Lading, which means that the goods have not been loaded when the Bill of Lading is issued, but are on the dock awaiting loading.

⑪ **Mate's receipt**: An acknowledgement of receipt of a consignment on board a carrying vessel. It is usually given to the Master so that he may sign the Bill of Lading.

⑫ **Negotiable B/L**: The B/L which can be transferable or assignable.

⑬ **Endorsement**: A signature on the reverse of a negotiable instrument made primarily for the purpose of transferring the holder's rights to another person.

⑭ **Blank**: Endorsement, an endorsement of an instrument which does not specify any person to whom payment is to be made, thus making the amount named in the instrument payable to any person who presents it without further endorsement.

⑮ **Customs clearance**: Completion of customs formalities when exporting or importing goods.

⑯ **Van**: The truck used for carrying the household goods.

⑰ **Van operator**: The driver often uses vehicle carrying household goods.

⑱ **Bill of Lading(B/L)**: A document evidencing the receipt of goods for shipment issued by a person engaged in the business of transporting or forwarding goods; all important and necessary pertinent information is found on a Bill of Lading.

⑲ **Contract**: An agreement, either written or verbal, between two parties.

⑳ **Shipper**: The person whose household goods are being moved.

㉑ **Irregular route carrier**: A carrier operating within a specified and defined territory, as set forth in the carrier's certificate, but not over specified route or routes between fixed termini. Our industry members are irregular route carriers.

㉒ **Joint rates**: A joint rate is a rate that applies over the lines or routes of two or more carriers and that is made by arrangement or agreement between such carriers evidenced by concurrence of power of attorney. Joint tariffs are those which contain joint rates.

㉓ **Packing list**: A list of products shipped by the vendor to be used to verify the items during the receiving process. This document does not have any pricing on it generally and should not be confused with an invoice.

㉔ **Individual shipper**: The owner of household goods being shipped.

㉕ **Interchange**: The exchange of freight laden trailers from one carrier to another for further-transportation of the shipments therein.

㉖ **Interline**: The transfer of a shipment from one carrier to another for further transportation.

㉗ **Interstate**: Move which has its origin and destination situated in different states. This alsoincludes moves which have origin and destination in the same state, but which pass through another state on their way.

㉘ **Carrier**: A company that transports passengers, freight or household goods.

㉙ **Cartons**: Containers used for packing smaller odds and ends. Breakables and non-breakables may be packed in cartons.

㉚ **Order number**: The number used to identify each shipment. It appears on both the Bill ofLading and the Order for Service.

㉛ **S. I. T. (Storage-In-Transit)**：Temporary storage of household goods in the warehouse of the carrier or his agent, pending further transportation.

㉜ **Inventory**：The detailed descriptive list of household goods showing number and condition of each item.

㉝ **Connecting flight**：A segment of on ongoing journey that requires passengers to change aircraft, but not necessarily carriers. Under International Air Transportation Association (IATA) regulations, a flight connection becomes a stopover if the passenger is required to wait more than 24 hours for the next flight.

（5）关于保险跟单的常见术语及解释

① **Marine insurance**：The insurance of ships or their cargo against specific causes of loss or damage that might be encountered at sea. The definition has been widened over the year to include the transit cargo over land at each end of the voyage.

② **Peril of the sea**：A marine insurance terms used to designate heavy weather, lighting, collision and sea water damage.

③ **Average**：In insurance, it means a loss, or the apportionment of a loss between different parties：general average refers to a loss incurred by one consignment, but shared by all the other consignors who use the same carrying vessel on the same voyage. Particular average refers to a partial loss of a consignment as a result of a hazard affecting only that the consignment and not a hazard affecting all the consignment on the same carrying vessel.

④ **Total loss**：Loss of the whole of a consignment.

⑤ **Partial loss**：The loss of part of goods.

⑥ **F.P.A.**：Abbreviation of "Free from Particular Average", an insurance term meaning that goods are covered only against hazards to which all the consignment on the same carrying vessel (or other means of transport) are subject, and not against hazards affecting only the insurer's consignment.

⑦ **W.P.A./H.W.A**：Short for "With Particular Average", an insurance term meaning that goods are covered against particular average.

⑧ **All Risks**：An insurance terms mean that the goods insured are covered against all the risks specified in the contract of insurance.

⑨ **Special risks**：Risks detailed in an insurance policy, over and above the normal cover afforded by that type of policy.

⑩ **Insurance policy**：A written document between an insured person and an insurance company specifying the exact losses to be covered and the costs to the insured person.

⑪ **Insurance certificate**：Document issued under, eg. an open cover policy, instead of a policy of insurance.

⑫ **Freight**：The compensation paid for the transportation of goods. The ordinary transportation of goods by a common carrier and distinguished from express shipments.

⑬ **Freight forwarder**：Common carrier who transports or provides transport of property by assembling or consolidation of shipments, performs break bulk or distributing operations in regard to such consolidated shipments and assumes responsibility for the transportation of such goods from point of receipt to point of destination.

⑭ **Customs**: The federal agency charged with collecting duty (taxes) on specific items imported into the country and restricting the entry of forbidden items.

⑮ **Customs broker**: A person or firm that specializes in international documentation and clearances.

2. General Catalog of E-commerce Platform 电子商务平台的产品目录及分类

C001 Electronics 数码电子产品

C001001 Computer & Networking C001 计算机 & 网络设备

C001001001 Tablets C001001 平板电脑

C001001002 Laptops C001001 笔记本电脑

C001001003 Desktops C001001 台式电脑

C001001004 Storage C001001 内存条

C001001005 Networking C001001 网络设备

C001001006 Tablet Accessories C001001 平板电脑配件

C001001007 Laptop Accessories C001001 笔记本电脑配件

C001001008 Computer Peripherals C001001 计算机外设

C001001009 Computer Components C001001 计算机部件

C001002 Consumer Electronics C001 消费电子产品

C001002001 Camera & Photography C001002 相机 & 摄影影器材

C001002002 Home Audio & Video C001002 家庭影音设备

C001002003 TV Stick C001002 电视网络播放器

C001002004 Accessories & Parts C001002 相关配件 & 部件

C001002005 Video Games C001002 游戏机 & 配件

C001002006 Portable Audio & Video C001002 便携式影音设备

C001002007 Earphones & Headphones C001002 耳机 & 头戴式耳机

C001002008 Mini Camcorders C001002 微型摄像机

C001002009 Memory Cards C001002 内存卡

C001003 Phones & Accessories C001 手机 & 配件

C001003001 Mobile Phones C001003 手机

C001003002 Bags & Cases C001003 手机套 & 手机壳

C001003003 Batteries C001003 电池

C001003004 Chargers & Docks C001003 充电器

C001003005 Backup Powers C001003 充电宝

C001003006 Cables C001003 数据线

C001003007 Lenses C001003 手机镜头

C001003008 Parts C001003 手机部件

C001003009 LCDS C001003 手机屏

C001003010 Holders & Stands C001003 手机座

C001003011 Stickers C001003 手机贴

C002 Apparel & Accessories 服装 & 配饰

C002001 Women C002 女装

C002001001 Dresses C00201 连衣裙

C002001002 Coats & Jackets C002001 大衣 & 外套

C00003 Blouses & Shirts C002001 上衣 & 衬衫

C002001004 Tops & Tees C002001 短袖 & T 恤

C002001005 Hoodies & Sweatshirts C002001 卫衣 & 运动衫

C002001006 Intimates C002001 内衣

C002001007 Swimwear C002001 泳衣

C002001008 Pants & Capris C002001 长裤 & 紧身裤

C002001009 Sweaters C002001 毛衣

C002001010 Skirts C002001 半身裙

C00200101 I Leggings C002001 打底裤

C002001012 Accessories C002001 配饰

C002002 Men C002 男装

C002002001 Tops & Tees C002002 短袖 &T 恤

C002002002 Coats & Jackets C002002 大衣 & 外套

C002002003 Underwear C002002 内衣

C002002004 Shirts C002002 衬衫

C002002005 Hoodies & Sweatshirts C002002 卫衣 & 运动衫

C002002006 Jeans C002002 牛仔裤

C002002007 Pants C000002 长裤

C002002008 Suits & Blazer C0020020 套装 & 西装

C002002009 Shorts C0020020 短裤

C002002010 Sweaters C0020020 毛衣

C002002011 Accessories C002002 配饰

C002003 Wedding & Events C002 婚礼 & 特殊场合礼服

C002003001 Wedding Dresses C002003 婚纱

C002003002 Evening Dresses C002003 晚礼服

C002003003 Homecoming Dresses C002003 校友返校日礼服

C002003004 Ball Gown C002003 舞会礼服

C002003005 Cocktail Dresses C002003 鸡尾酒会礼服

C002003006 Casual Party Dresses C002003 聚会礼服

C002003007 Celebrity-Inspired Dresses C002003 明星款礼服

C002003008 Quinceanera Dresses C002003 成人礼礼服

C002003009 Communion Dresses C002003 圣餐礼服

C002003010 Graduation Dresses C002003 毕业礼服

C002003011 Wedding Accessorizes C002003 婚纱配饰

C002003012 Wedding Party Dress C002003 婚礼礼服

C003 Bags & Shoes 箱包 & 鞋子

C003001 Luggage Bags C003 行李箱 & 包

C003001001 Women's Shoulder Bags C003001 女式单肩包

C003001002 Women's Wallets C003001 女式钱包

C003001003 Women's Crossbody Bags C003001 女式长带包

C003001004 Women's Totes C003001 女式手提包

C003001005 Women's Clutches C003001 女士手包

C003001006 Women's Backpacks C003001 女式双肩包

C003001007 Men's Wallets C003001 男式钱包

C003001008 Men's Backpacks C003001 男式双肩包

C003001009 Men's Briefcases C003001 男式公文包

C003001010 Men's Crossbody Bags C003001 男式长带包

C003001011 School Bags C003001 书包

C003001012 Travel Duffle C003001 旅行包

C003002 Shoes C003 鞋子

C003002001 Women's Fashion Sneakers C003002 女式帆布鞋

C003002002 Women's Sandals C003002 女式凉鞋

C003002003 Women's Flats C003002 女式平底鞋

C003002004 Women's Pumps C003002 高跟鞋

C003002005 Women's Boots C003002 女靴

C003002006 Women's Slippers C003002 女式拖鞋

C003002007 Men's Fashion Sneakers C003002 男式帆布鞋

C003002008 Men's Flats C003002 男式平底鞋

C003002009 Men's Sandals C003002 男式凉鞋

C003002010 Men's Boots C003002 男靴

C003002011 Men's Loafers C003002 男式便鞋

C003002012 Men's Slippers C003002 男式拖鞋

C003003 Children's Shoes C003 童鞋

C003003001 Girls' Sneakers C003003 平底女童鞋

C003003002 Boys' Sneakers C003003 平底男童鞋

C003003003 Girls' Sandals C003003 女童凉鞋

C003003004 Boys' Sandals C003003 男童凉鞋

C003003005 Children's Boots C003003 童靴

C003000 Girls' Leather Shoes C003003 女童皮鞋

C003003007 Boys' Leather Shoes C003003 男童皮鞋

C003003008 Baby First Walkers C003003 学步鞋

C003003009 Baby Leather Shoes C003003 婴儿皮鞋

C003003010 Baby Sneakers C003003 婴儿平底鞋

C003003011 Baby Boots C003003 婴儿靴

C003003012 Baby Sandals C003003 婴儿凉鞋

C004 Home & Garden 家居 & 园艺

C004001 Home & Garden C004 家居用品

C004001001 Home Decor C004001 家居饰品

C004001002 Home Textile C004001 家纺

C004001003 Kitchen，Dining & Bar C004001 厨具、餐具 & 酒具

C004001004 Bathroom Products C004001 卫浴用品

C004001005 Festive & Party Supplies C004001 节日 & 聚会用品

C004001006 Home Storage & Organization C004001 收纳用品

C004001007 Household Cleaning Tools & Accessories C004001 清洁用品

C004001008 Pet Products C004001 宠物用品

C004001009 Bedding Set C004001 床上用品

C004001010 Curtains C004001 窗帘带

C004001011 Painting & Calligraphy C004001 装饰书画

C004001012 Furniture C004001 家具 & 配件

C004002 Outdoors & Garden C004 户外 & 花园用品

C004002001 Garden Pots & Planters C004002 花盆

C004002002 Garden Landscaping & Decking C004002 花园造景 & 美化

C004002003 Garden Tools C004002 园艺工具

C004002004 Watering & Irrigation C004002 浇水灌溉用具

C004002005 Temperature Gauges C004002 温度计 & 测温仪

C004002006 Fertilizer C004002 花肥

C004002007 BBQC004002 烧烤用具

C004002008 Shade C004002 遮阳用具

C004002009 Mailboxes C0040002 信箱

C004002010 Garden-Buildings C004002 篱笆 & 温室

C004002011 Outdoor Furniture C004002 户外家具

C004002012 Bonsai C004002 盆景

C004003 Home Improvement C004 灯具 & 杂货

C004003001 Lighting C004003 灯具

C004003002 Home Security C004003 家用安全装置

C004003003 Home Appliances C004003 小家电

C004003004 Hardware C004003 小五金件

C004003005 Hand Tools C004003 家用小工具

C004003006 Kitchen & Bath Fixtures C004003 厨房 & 卫浴设施

C004003007 Faucets. Mixers & Taps C004003 水龙头 & 花酒

C004003008 CCTV Product CO04003 闭路电视设备

C004003009 Indoor Lighting C004003 室内灯具

C004003010 Outdoor Lighting C004003 室外灯具

C004003011 Lighting Bulbs & Tubes C004003 灯泡 & 灯管

C004003012 LED Lighting C004003LED 灯具

C005 Toys, Kids & Baby 玩具 & 婴幼用品

C005001 Clothing & Accessories C005 童装 & 配饰

C005001001 Girls C005001 女童装

C005001002 Boys C005001 男童装

C005001003 Baby Girls C005001 女婴装

C005001004 Baby Boys C005001 男婴装

C005001005 Clothing Sets C005001 童装套装

C005001006 Girls' Dress C005001 女童连衣裙

C005001007 Boys' T-shirts C005001 男童 T 恤

C005001008 Baby Rompers C005001 幼儿背带裤

C005001009 Children's School Bags C000001 儿童书包

C005001010 Baby First Walkers C005001 学步鞋

C005001011 Children's Shoes C005001 儿童鞋

C005001012 Children's Accessories C005001 儿童配饰

C005002 Toys C005 玩具

C005002001 Stuffed Animals & Plush C005002 毛线玩具

C005002002 RC Helicopters C005002 遥控玩具直升机

C005002003 Action Figures C005002 卡通人偶玩具

C005002004 Balloons C005002 气球

C005002005 Model Building C005002 拼装玩具

C005002006 Blocks CO05002 积木玩具

C005002007 Dolls Accessories C005002 洋娃娃配饰

C00S002008 Electronic Toys C005002 电子玩具

C005002009 Learning & Education C05002 益智玩具

C005002010 Baby Toys C005002 婴儿玩具

C005002011 Outdoor Fun & Sports C005002 户外玩具体育用品

C005003 Baby & Maternity Products C005 母婴用品

C005003001 Nappy Changing C005003 妈咪包

C005003002 Activity & Gear C005003 出行用品

C005003003 Baby Care C005003 婴儿护理

C005003004 Safety Gear C005003 安全用品

C005003005 Feeding C005003 喂（吸）养用品

C005003006 Bedding C005003 婴儿床上用品

C005003007 Swimming Pool C005003 儿游冰池

C005003008 Baby Monitors C005003 婴儿监视器

C005003009 Maternity Dress C005003 孕妇裙

C005003010 Intimates C005003 孕妇内衣

C005003011 Maternity Tops C005003 孕妇上衣

C006 Automotive 汽车

C006001 Car Electronics C006 车用电子产品

C006001001 Motor Electronics C006001 车用小电子产品

C006001002 Car DVD C006001 车载 DVD

C006001003 Alarm Systems & Security C006001 报警系统 & 安全装置

C006001004 DVR/Camera C006001 行车记录仪

C006001005 Radar Detectors C006001 测速仪

C006001006 GPS C006001 GPS 导航仪

C006001007 Car Video Players C006001 车载播放器

C006001008 Motorcycle C006001 摩托车用品

C006001009 Motorbike Brakes C006001 摩托制车片

C006001010 Protective Gears C006001 摩托车手保护装备

C06001011 Electrical System C006001 摩托车电气装置

C006002 Replacement Parts C006 汽车配件

C006002001 Car Parts C006002 汽车部件

C006002002 Car Lights C006002 车灯

C006002003 External Lights C006002 外灯

C006002004 Car Light Source C006002 车用 LED 灯

C006002005 Interior Lights C0060002 内灯

C006002006 Engine C0006002 引擎

C006002007 Fuel Injector 0002 喷油嘴

C006002008 Car Accessories C006002 汽车配件

C006002009 Car Stickers C006002 车饰

C006002010 Chromium Styling C006002 车身保护条

C006002011 Bumpers C006002 保险杠保护条

C006002012 Car Covers C006002 车罩

C006003 Tools & Maintenance C006 汽车保养工具

C006003001 Tools & Equipment C006003 车用工具 & 装置

C006003002 Diagnostic Tools C006003 汽车诊断仪

C006003003 Code Readers & Scan Tools C006003 汽车扫描仪

C006003004 Car Washer C006003 洗车用具

C006003005 Car Chargers C006003 车载充电器

C006003006 Steering Covers C006003 方向盘套

C006003007 Seat Covers C006003 汽车座套

C006003008 Floor Mats C006003 汽车置物防滑垫

C007 Sports & Outdoor 运动 & 户外

C007001 Sports Clothing C007 运动服装

C007001001 Hiking Jackets C007001 登山服

C007001002 Hiking T-Shirts C007001 登山 T 恤

C007001003 Hiking Pants C007001 登山长裤

C007001004 Rucksacks C007001 登山包

C007001005 Running T-Shirts C007001 跑步 T 恤

C007001006 Running Bags C007001 跑步包

C007001007 Cycling Jersey C007001 自行车骑行服

C007001008 Cycling Jackets C007001 自行车骑行外套

C007001009 Cycling Shorts C007001 自行车骑行短裤

C007001010 Cycling Eyewear C007001 自行车骑行眼镜

C007001011 Skiing Jackets C007001 滑雪服

C007001012 Soccer Jersey C007001 足球衣

C007002 Sport Shoes C007 运动鞋

C007002001 Running Shoes C007002 跑步鞋

C007002002 Basketball Shoes C007002 篮球鞋

C007002003 Soccer Shoes C007002 足球鞋

C007002004 Hiking Shoes C007002 登山鞋

C007002005 Skateboarding Shoes C007002 滑板鞋

C007002006 Tennis Shoes C007002 网球鞋

C007002007 Walking Shoes C007002 健走鞋

C007002008 Dance Shoes C007002 舞鞋

C007002009 Skate Shoes C007002 轮滑鞋

C007002010 Fitness Shoes C007002 健身鞋

C007003 Sport Equipment C007 运动装备

C007003001 Bicycle C007003 自行车

C007003002 Bicycle Parts C007003 自行车部件

C007003003 Bicycle Helmet C007003 自行车头盔

C007003004 Bicycle Light C007003 自行车灯

C007003005 Bicycle Bags & Panniers C00003 自行车骑输行包 & 车筐

C007003006 Fishing Reels C007003 鱼线轮

C007003007 Fishing Rods C007003 钓竿

C007003008 Fishing Lines C007003 鱼线

C007003009 Fishing Lures C007003 鱼饵

C007003010 Tent C007003 帐篷

C007003011 Yoga C007003 瑜伽用品

C007003012 Guitar C007003 吉他

C008 Jewelry & Watches 首饰 & 手表

C008001 Fashion Jewelry C008 时尚饰品

C008001001 Necklaces & Pendants C008001 项链 & 吊坠

C008001002 Bracelets & Bangles C0008001 手镯 & 手链

C008001003 Earrings C008001 耳饰

C00800104 Rings C008001 戒指

C008001005 Jewelry Sets C008001 首饰

C008001006 Hair Jewelry C008001 发饰

C008001007 Tie Clips Cufflinks C008001 领带夹 & 袖口

C008001008 Brooches C008001 胸针

C008001009 Charms C008001 小饰品

C008001010 Body Jewelry C008001 鼻饰 & 肚脐饰品

C008001011 Anklets C008001 脚链

C008001012 Jewelry Findings Components C008001 饰品小配件

C008002 Watches C008 手表

C00800200 Sports Watches C008002 运动手表

C008002002 Wristwatches C008002 腕表

C008002003 Fashion Casual Watches C008002 时尚休闲手表

C008002004 Pocket & Fob Watches C008002 怀表

C008002005 Women's Fashion Watches C008002 女式时尚手表

C00800206 Men's Casual Watches C008002 男士休闲手表

C008002007 Lover's Wristwatches C008002 情侣手表

C008002008 Watch Accessories C00802 手表配件

C008003 Fine Jewelry C008 高档首饰

C008003001 Diamond Series C0080003 钻石首饰

C008003002 Pearl Collection C008003 珍珠首饰

C008003003 Ruby Jewelry C008003 红宝石首饰

C008003004 Sapphire Jewelry C008003 蓝宝石首饰

C008003005 Silver C008003 银饰

C008003006 Necklaces Pendants C008003 项链表吊坠

C008003007 Rings C008003 戒指

C008003008 Earrings C008003 耳饰

C00030090 Jewelry Sets C008003 首饰套装

C008003010 Charms C008003 小饰品

C008003011 Bracelets & Bangles C008003 手镯 & 手链

C009 Beauty & Health 美容美发 & 保健

C009001 Beauty C009 美发

C009001001 Hair Styling C009001 美发用品

C009001002 Hair Rollers C009001 卷发器

C009001003 Straightening Irons C009001 直发器

C009001004 Hair Trimmers C009000 电动理发器

C009001005 Hair Dryers C00900 吹风机

C009001006 Hair Scissors C009001 理发剪刀

C009001007 Hair Color C009001 一次性染发粉

C009001008 Hair Loss Products C009001 头发生长精华素

C009001009 Shaving & Hair Removal C009001 剃须 & 脱毛用品

C009001010 Combs C009001 梳子

C009001011 Mirrors C009001 镜子

C009002 Hair C009 假发

C009002001 Human Hair C009002 真发制假发

C009002002 Hair Weaves C00002 织发补发片

C009002003 Hair Extension C009002 驳发

C009002004 Wigs C009002 假发片

C009002005 Closure C009002 一片式假发

C009002006 Synthetic Hair C009002 合成纤维假发

C009008007 Blended Hair C00902 真发与合成纤维混合制假发

C009002008 Feather Hair C009002 羽毛假发

C009002009 Accessories Tools C00002 假发配件 & 工具

C009003 Additional Categories C009 美容用品及其他

C009003001 Makeup C009003 美妆用品

C009003002 Nail & Tools C009003 美甲用品

C009003003 Skin Care C009003 护肤用品

C009003004 Health Care C009003 保健用品

C009003005 Oral Hygiene C009003 口腔保健

C009003006 Tattoo Body Art C009003 纹身用品

C009003007 Sex Products C009003 成人用品

C009003008 Fragrances & Deodorants C009003 香水 & 香体露

C009003009 Bath & Shower C009003 沐浴用品

C009003010 Sanitary Paper C009003 尿片

3. Trade-related Basic Information of the World by Country 世界部分国家和地区贸易相关基础信息

具体见附表1。

附表1 世界各国贸易相关基础信息（2017年）

Trade-related Basic Information of the World by Country（as of 2017）

A	国际长途区号（Country Code）
B	货币代码与符号（Currency Code and symbol）
C	汇率（Exchange Rate） 注:请查阅最新数据
D	时差（与中国）Time difference with China（in hour）
E	人口（百万）[Population（in million）]
F	GDP 排名（GDP Ranking） 注:请查阅最新数据
G	主要港口（Main Sea Ports）
H	主要语言（Major Languages）

洲 Continent	国家或地区 Country or Area	A	B	C	D	E	F	G	H
亚洲 Asia	中国大陆 mainland China	86	CNY ¥	1	0	1,400	2	上海、广州 Shanghai, Guangzhou	中文 Chiense
亚洲 Asia	日本 Japan	81	JPY ¥	16.99	1	127	3	东京、广岛 Tokyo, Hiroshima	日语 Japanese
亚洲 Asia	马来西亚 Malaysia	60	MYR	0.62	0	29.9	39	巴生港、丹戎帕拉帕斯港 Port Klang, PortTanjung Pelepas	马来语 Bahasa Melayu
亚洲 Asia	菲律宾 Philippines	63	PHP	6.58	0	100	40	马尼拉、宿务 Manila, Cebu	塔加洛语 Tagalog
亚洲 Asia	泰国 Thailand	66	THB	5.07	1	68.86	26	曼谷、林查班 Bangkok, Leam Chabang	泰语 Thai
亚洲 Asia	越南 Vietnam	84	VND	3521.1	1	92.7	48	海防港、胡志明港 Haiphong, Hochiminh	越南语 Vietnamese
亚洲 Asia	中国香港 Hong Kong, China	852	HKD	1.21	0	7.41	35	香港 Hong Kong	粤语 Cantonese

洲 Continent	国家或地区 Country or Area	A	B	C	D	E	F	G	H
亚洲 Asia	柬埔寨 Cambodia	855	KHR	610.46	1	15.76	103	磅逊、金边 Kompong Som、 Phnom Penh	柬埔寨语 Cambodia
亚洲 Asia	孟加拉国 Bangladesh	880	BDT	12.75	2	163	46	吉大港、达卡 Chittagon、Dhaka	孟加拉语 Bengali
亚洲 Asia	印度 India	91	INR	10.67	2.5	1324	6	新德里、孟买 New Delhi、Mumbai	印地语 Hindi
亚洲 Asia	阿富汗 Afghanistan	93	AFN	0.154	3	34.66	106	喀布尔、安其内 Aqineh、Kabul	普什图语 Pashto
亚洲 Asia	缅甸 Myanmar	95	MMK	212.45	1.5	52.89	74	仰光、勃生 Yangon、Bessein	缅甸语 Burmese
亚洲 Asia	黎巴嫩 Lebanon	961	LBP	231.8	6	6.7	81	贝鲁特、舍卡 Beirut、Chekka	阿拉伯语 Arbic
亚洲 Asia	叙利亚 Syria	963	SYP	80.67	6	18.43	68	巴尼亚斯、拉塔基亚 Banias、Lattakia	阿拉伯语 Arbic
亚洲 Asia	科威特 Kuwait	965	KWD	0.05	5	4.24	59	霍尔姆法塔、科威特 Khor Al Mufatta、 Kuwait	阿拉伯语 Arbic
亚洲 Asia	阿曼 Oman	968	OMR	0.06	4	4.4	75	费赫勒港、米纳卡布斯 Mina Al Fahal、 Mina Qaboos	阿拉伯语 Arbic
亚洲 Asia	巴林 Bahrain	973	BHD	0.06	5	1.4	98	奥巴杰蒂、 米纳苏尔曼 Albajetty、 Mina Sulman	阿拉伯语 Arbic
亚洲 Asia	阿联酋 UAE	971	AED	0.58	4	9.27	32	迪拜、阿布扎比 Dubai、Abu Dhabi	阿拉伯语 Arbic
亚洲 Asia	不丹 Bhutan	975	BTN	9.8	2	0.8	151		宗卡语 Dzongkha

续表

洲 Continent	国家或地区 Country or Area	A	B	C	D	E	F	G	H
亚洲 Asia	尼泊尔 Nepal	977	NPR	17.01	2.25	28.98	98		尼泊尔语 Nepali
亚洲 Asia	塞浦路斯 Cuprus	357	EUR €	0.13	6	1.17	104	利马索尔、 阿莫霍斯托斯 Limassol , Ammochostus	希腊语 Greek
亚洲 Asia	印度尼西亚 Indonesia	62	IDR	2219.9	1	261.1	16	雅加达、勿拉湾 Jakarta , Belawan	印尼语 Bahasa Indonesia
亚洲 Asia	新加坡 Singapore	65	SGD	0.21	0	5.67	38	新加坡港、 普劳布科姆 Singapore , Pulau Bukom	英语 English
亚洲 Asia	文莱 Brunei	673	BND	0.21	0	0.42	121	斯里巴加湾港、 白拉奕 Bandar Seri Begawan , Kuala Belait	马来语 Bahasa Melayu
亚洲 Asia	韩国 South Korea	82	KRW	169.11	1	51.45	11	首尔、釜山 Seoul , Busan	韩语 Korean
亚洲 Asia	朝鲜 North Korea	850	KPW	141.13	1	25.369	152	清津、南浦 Chungjin , Nampo	朝鲜语 Korean
亚洲 Asia	中国澳门 Macao , China	853	MOP	1.27	0	0.65	85	澳门 Macao	粤语 Cantonese
亚洲 Asia	老挝 Laos	856	LAK	1307.9	1	6.76	111		老挝语 Laotian
亚洲 Asia	中国台湾 Taiwan , China	886	TWD	4.67	0	23.49	22	高雄、基隆 Kaohsiung , Keelung	闽南语 SouthernFujian Dialect
亚洲 Asia	土耳其 Turkey	90	TRY	0.72	5	7.95	18	伊兹米尔、 伊斯坦布尔 Izmir , Istanbul	土耳其语 Turkic
亚洲 Asia	巴基斯坦 Pakistan	92	PKR	18.08	3	190.3	42	卡拉奇、卡西姆 Karachi , Qasim	乌尔都语 Urdu

洲 Continent	国家或地区 Country or Area	A	B	C	D	E	F	G	H
亚洲 Asia	斯里兰卡 Sri lanka	94	LKR	24.44	2.5	21.2	67	科伦坡、加勒 Colombo、Galle	僧伽罗语 Sinhalese
亚洲 Asia	马尔代夫 Maldives	960	MVR	1.88	3	0.42	150	马累岛、阿杜环礁 Male、Addu atoll	迪维希语 Dhivehi
亚洲 Asia	约旦 Jordan	962	JOD	9.1527	6	9.456	86	亚喀巴、安曼 Aqaba、Amman	阿拉伯语 Arbic
亚洲 Asia	伊拉克 Irap	964	IQD	181.92	5	31.23	48	法奥、巴士拉 Fao、Basrah	阿拉伯语 Arbic
亚洲 Asia	沙特阿拉伯 Saudi Arabia	966	SAR	1.7	5	32.28	20	吉达、达曼 Jeddah、Dammam	阿拉伯语 Arbic
亚洲 Asia	以色列 Israel	972	ILS	0.56	6	8.54	37	埃拉特、阿什杜德 Eilat、Ashdod	阿拉伯语 Arbic
亚洲 Asia	卡塔尔 Qatar	974	QAR	0.56	5	2.57	45	多哈、哈卢勒岛 Doha、Halul Island	阿拉伯语 Arbic
亚洲 Asia	蒙古 Mongolian	976	MNT	375.5	0	3.02	118		蒙古语 Mongolian language
亚洲 Asia	伊朗 Iran	98	IRR	5278.6	4.5	80.277	27	布什尔、霍梅尼港 Bushire、 Bandar Khomeini	波斯语 Persian
亚洲 Asia	也门 Yemen	967	YER	37.58	5	27.58	82	亚丁、荷台达 Aden、Hodeidah	阿拉伯语 Arbic
亚洲 Asia	哈萨克斯坦 Kazakhstan	7	KZT	51.57	2	17.797	50	阿克套、阿克托别 Aktau、Aktobe	哈萨克语 Kazakh
亚洲 Asia	乌兹别克斯坦 Uzbekistan	998	UZS	0.15	3	31.85	67	撒马尔罕、喀什 Samarcant、Karshi	乌兹别克语 Uzbek
亚洲 Asia	塔吉克斯坦 Tajikistan	992	TJS	1.389	3	8.73	134	杜尚别、苦盏 Dushanbe、Khujand	塔吉克语 Tajik

洲 Continent	国家或地区 Country or Area	A	B	C	D	E	F	G	H
亚洲 Asia	土库曼斯坦 Tukmenistan	993	TMT	0.15	3	5.66	76	阿什哈巴德、 土库曼巴希 Ashgabat, Cahrgo Turkmenabad	土库曼语 Turkmen
亚洲 Asia	格鲁吉亚 Georigia	995	GEL	0.38	4	3.72	109	巴塔米、波季 Batumi, Poti	格鲁吉亚语 Georgian
亚洲 Asia	吉尔吉斯斯坦 Kyrgyzstan	996	KGS	10.486	2	6.08	136	奥什、比什凯克 Osh, Bisheke	俄语 Russian
亚洲 Asia	亚美尼亚 Armenia	374	AMD	74.127	4	2.92	126	埃里温 Yerevan	亚美尼亚语 Armenian
亚洲 Asia	阿塞拜疆 Azerbaijan	994	AZN	0.154	4	9.76	70	巴库 Baku	阿塞拜疆语 Azeri
欧洲 Europe	德国 Germany	49	EUR €	7.58	7	82.67	4	汉堡、不莱梅 Hamburg, Bremen	德语 German language
欧洲 Europe	法国 France	33	EUR €	7.85	7	66.89	5	福斯、勒阿弗尔 Fos, Lehavre	法语 French
欧洲 Europe	英国 Britain	44	GBP £	8.63	8	65.63	6	弗里克斯托、 南安普顿 Felixstowe, Southampton	英语 English
欧洲 Europe	意大利 Italy	39	EUR €	7.85	7	60.6	9	热那亚、威尼斯 Genova, Venezia	意大利语 Italian
欧洲 Europe	俄罗斯 Russian	7	RUB ₽	9.94	6	140.33	14		俄语 Russian
欧洲 Europe	西班牙 Spain	34	EUR €	7.85	7	46.44	14	维哥、巴伦西亚 Vigo, Valencia	西班牙语 Spanish
欧洲 Europe	荷兰 Holand	31	EUR €	7.85	7	170.2	18	鹿特丹 Rotterdam	荷兰语 Dutch
欧洲 Europe	瑞士 Switzerland	41	CHF	0.15	7	8.37	19	巴塞尔、苏黎世 Basel, Zurich	德语 German language

续表

洲 Continent	国家或地区 Country or Area	A	B	C	D	E	F	G	H
欧洲 Europe	瑞典 Sweden	46	SEK	1.36	7	9.9	23	奥胡斯、阿拉 Ahus , Ala	瑞典语 Swedish
欧洲 Europe	波兰 Poland	48	PLN	0.57	7	37.95	24	达尔沃沃、格但斯克 Darlowo , Gdansk	波兰语 Polish language
欧洲 Europe	比利时 Belgium	32	EUR €	7.85	7	11.35	25	安特卫普、布鲁日 Antwerp , Bruges	荷兰语 Dutch
欧洲 Europe	奥地利 Austria	43	EUR €	7.85	7	8.75	28	格拉茨、萨尔斯堡 Graz , Salzburg	德语 German language
欧洲 Europe	挪威 Norway	47	NOK	1.24	7	5.23	30	奥勒松、卑尔根 Alesund , Bergen	挪威语 Norergian
欧洲 Europe	爱尔兰 Ireland	353	EUR €	7.85	8	4.77	35	阿洛克、巴利纳 Arklow , Ballina	爱尔兰语 Irish
欧洲 Europe	丹麦 Denmark	45	DKK	0.98	7	5.73	36	奥本罗、奥尔堡 Aabenraa , Aalborg	丹麦语 Danish
欧洲 Europe	芬兰 Finland	358	EUR €	7.85	6	5.5	42	巴罗生特、代格比 Barosund , Degerby	芬兰语 Finnish
欧洲 Europe	葡萄牙 Portuguesa	351	EUR €	7.85	8	10.32	46	阿威罗、巴雷鲁 Aveiro , Barreiro	葡萄牙语 Portuguese
欧洲 Europe	捷克 Czech	420	CZK	3.4	7	10.56	48	布拉格 Prague	捷克语 Czech
欧洲 Europe	希腊 Greece	30	EUR €	7.85	6	10.75	49	哈尔基斯、干尼亚 Chalkis , Canea	希腊语 Greek
欧洲 Europe	匈牙利 Hungary	36	HUF	42.827	7	9.81	55	布达佩斯 Budapest	匈牙利语 Hungarian
欧洲 Europe	乌克兰 Ukraine	380	UAN	0.26	6	45	60	雅尔塔、尤日内 Yalta , Yuzhnyy	乌克兰语 Ukrainian
欧洲 Europe	斯洛伐克 Slovakia	421	EUR €	7.85	7	5.43	63	布拉迪斯拉发 Bratislava	斯洛伐克语 Slovakia

续表

洲 Continent	国家或地区 Country or Area	A	B	C	D	E	F	G	H
欧洲 Europe	卢森堡 Luxemburg	352	EUR €	7.85	7	0.58	72	卢森堡 Luxemburg	卢森堡语 Luxembourgish
欧洲 Europe	保加利亚 Bulgaria	359	BGN	0.26	6	7.13	75	巴尔奇克、布加斯 Balchik, Bourgas	保加利亚语 Bulgarian
欧洲 Europe	克罗地亚 Croatia	385	HRK	0.97	7	4.17	76	巴卡尔、奥米什 Bakar, Dugirat	克罗地亚语 Croatia
欧洲 Europe	白俄罗斯 Belarus	375	BYR	0.31	6	9.57	77	明斯克 Minsk	白俄罗斯语 Belarus
欧洲 Europe	斯洛文尼亚 Slovenia	386	EUR €	7.85	7	2.06	81	科佩尔、伊佐拉 Koper, Izola	斯洛文尼亚语 Slovenia
欧洲 Europe	立陶宛 Lithuania	370	EUR €	7.85	6	2.87	82	克莱佩达、考纳斯 Klaipeda, Kaunas	立陶宛语 Lithuania
欧洲 Europe	拉托维亚 Latvia	371	EUR €	7.85	6	19.6	93	利耶帕亚、 文茨皮尔斯 Liepaja, Ventspils	拉托维亚语 Latvia
欧洲 Europe	爱沙尼亚 Estonia	372	EUR €	7.85	6	1.32	97	派尔努、塔林 Parnu, Tallinn	爱沙尼亚语 Estonia
欧洲 Europe	冰岛 Lceland	354	ISK	16.65	8	0.33	100	阿克拉内斯、 阿克雷里 Akranes, Akureyri	冰岛语 Lceland
欧洲 Europe	阿尔巴尼亚 Albania	355	ALL	0.15	7	2.88	119	都拉斯 Durres	阿尔巴尼亚语 Albanian
欧洲 Europe	马耳他 Malta	356	EUR €	7.85	7	0.44	123	瓦莱塔、 马尔萨什洛克 Valletta, Marsaxlokk	马耳他语 Maltese
欧洲 Europe	摩尔多瓦 Moldova	373	MDL	0.38	6	3.55	136	基希讷乌 Chisinau	摩尔多瓦语 Moldavian
欧洲 Europe	圣马力诺 San Marino	223	EUR €	7.85	7	0.03	162	塞拉瓦莱 Serravalle	意大利语 Italian

续表

洲 Continent	国家或地区 Country or Area	A	B	C	D	E	F	G	H
美洲 America	美国 United States of America	1	USD $	0.154	12	323.1	1	纽约、洛杉矶 New York, Los Angeles	英语 English
美洲 America	巴西 Brazil	55	BRL	0.32	11	208	9	阿里亚布兰卡、 安格拉杜斯雷斯 Areia Branca, Angra Dos Reis	葡萄牙语 Portuguese
美洲 America	加拿大 Canada	1	CAD C$	0.204	11	36.28	10	温哥华、哈利法克斯 Vancouver, Halifax	英语 English
美洲 America	墨西哥 Mexico	52	MXN	3.0758	14	128	15	墨西哥城、曼萨尼略 Mexico City, Manzanillo	西班牙语 Spanish
美洲 America	阿根廷 Argentina	54	ARS	4.151	11	43.85	21	布宜诺斯艾利斯 、 布兰卡港 Buenos Aires, Bahia Blanca	西班牙语 Spanish
美洲 America	哥伦比亚 Colombia	57	COP	448.03	13	48.6	39	布埃纳文图拉、 圣玛尔塔 Buenaventura, Santa Marta	西班牙语 Spanish
美洲 America	智利 Chile	56	CLP	98.135	12	17	41	瓦尔帕莱索港、 圣安东尼奥港 Valparaiso, San Antonio	西班牙语 Spanish
美洲 America	秘鲁 Peru	51	PEN	0.502	13	31.77	51	卡亚俄港、钱凯 Callao, Chancay	西班牙语 Spanish
美洲 America	委内瑞拉 Venezuela	58	VEF	12277	12	31.568	54	拉瓜伊拉、卡贝略港 La Guaira, Puerto Cabello	西班牙语 Spanish
美洲 America	厄瓜多尔 Ecuador	593	ECS	3982.5	13	16.39	59	瓜亚基尔、 埃斯梅拉达斯 Guayaquil, Esmeraldas	西班牙语 Spanish

洲 Continent	国家或地区 Country or Area	A	B	C	D	E	F	G	H
美洲 America	危地马拉 Guatemala	502	GTQ	1.151	14	16.58	71	巴里奥斯港、圣何塞 Puerto Barrios, Puerto Quetzal	西班牙语 Spanish
美洲 America	乌拉圭 Uruguay	598	UYU	4.865	11	3.4	74	蒙得维的亚、 科洛尼亚 Montevideo, Colonia	西班牙语 Spanish
美洲 America	巴拿马 Panama	507	PAB	0.153	13	4	77	巴拿马城 Panama City	西班牙语 Spanish
美洲 America	玻利维亚 Bolivia	591	BOB	1.055	12	10.89	87	科恰班巴、拉巴斯 Cochabamba, Ia Paz	西班牙语 Spanish
美洲 America	巴拉圭 Paraguay	595	PYG	872.11	12	6.73	92	亚松森、卡库佩米 Asuncion, Caacupemi	西班牙语 Spanish
美洲 America	特立尼达和多巴哥 Trinidad and Tobago	1-868	TTD	1.037	12	1.36	94	福廷角、利萨斯角 Point fortin, Point lisas	英语 English
美洲 America	萨尔瓦多 Salvador	503	SVC	1.32	14	6.345	96	阿卡胡特拉、 圣萨尔瓦多 Acajutla, San salvador	西班牙语 Spanish
美洲 America	洪都拉斯 Honduras	504	HNL	3.54	14	9.113	101	卡斯蒂利亚港、 科尔特斯港 Puerto castilla, Puerto cortes	西班牙语 Spanish
美洲 America	牙买加 Jamaica	876	JMD	20.09	13	2.8	114	金斯敦、蒙特歌湾 Kingston, Montego Bay	英语 English
美洲 America	尼加拉瓜 Nicaragua	505	NIO	4.85	14	6.15	116	科林托、马那瓜 Corinto, Managua	西班牙语 Spanish
美洲 America	巴哈马 Bahamas	242	BSD	0.15	12	0.39	131	弗里波特、拿骚 Freeport, Nassau	英语 English

洲 Continent	国家或地区 Country or Area	A	B	C	D	E	F	G	H
美洲 America	海地 Haiti	509	HTG	10.214	13	10.85	132	海地角、太子港 Cap Haitien Port Au Prince	法语 French
美洲 America	苏里南 Suriname	597	SRD	1.14	11	0.558	140	帕拉马里博、蒙戈 Paramaribo, Moengo	荷兰语 Dutch
美洲 America	巴巴多斯 Barbados	268	BBD	0.307	12	0.2849	146	巴巴多斯、布里奇敦 Barbados, Bridgetown	英语 English
美洲 America	圭亚那 Guyana	592	GYD	31.72	12	0.773	148	乔治敦、圭亚那 Georgetown gy, Guyana	英语 English
美洲 America	伯利兹 Belize	501	BZD	0.307	14	0.37	156	伯利兹 Belize City	英语 English
美洲 America	圣卢西亚 Saint Luica	1-758	XCD	0.415	12	0.178	159	卡斯特里、圣卢西亚 Castries, St.Lucia	英语 English
美洲 America	安提瓜和巴布达 Antigua and Barbuda	268	XCD	0.415	12	0.1009	162	安地卡、圣约翰斯 Antigua, St.Johns.Ag	英语 English
美洲 America	格林纳达 Grenada	473	XCD	0.415	12	0.1073	164	圣乔治、格林纳达 St.Georges, Grenada	英语 English
美洲 America	圣基茨和尼维斯 The Federation of Saint Kitts and Nevis	1 -869	XCD	0.415	12	0.0548	165	圣基茨岛、尼维斯 St.Kitts, Nevis	英语 English
美洲 America	圣文森特和 格林纳丁斯 Saint Vincent and the Grenadines	784	XCD	0.415	12	0.1096	168	圣文森特、金斯敦 Kingston, St.Vincent	英语 English
美洲 America	多米尼克 Dominica	1767	XCD	0.415	12	0.0735	171	多米尼克、罗索 Dominica, Roseau	英语 English

续表

洲 Continent	国家或地区 Country or Area	A	B	C	D	E	F	G	H
美洲 America	多米尼加 The Dominican Republic	1849	DOP	7.589	12	10.65	68	考塞多、普拉塔港 Caucedo, Puerto Plata	西班牙语 Spanish
大洋洲 Oceania	澳大利亚 Australia	61	AUD A$	0.201	2	24.13	13	悉尼、墨尔本 Sydney, Melbourne	英语 English
大洋洲 Oceania	新西兰 New Zealand	64	NZD	0.217	4	4.69	53	奥克兰、惠灵顿 Auckland, Wellington	英语 English
大洋洲 Oceania	巴布亚新几内亚 Papua New Guinea	675	PGK	0.498	2	8.08	105	莱城、莫尔兹比港 Lae, Port Moresby	英语 English
大洋洲 Oceania	斐济 Fiji	679	FJD	0.32	4	0.899	143	埃灵顿、劳托卡 Ellington, Lautoka	英语 English
大洋洲 Oceania	所罗门群岛 Solomon Islands	677	SBD	1.21	3	0.599	161	霍尼亚拉、阿拉迪斯港 Honiara, Allardyce Harbour	英语 English
大洋洲 Oceania	西萨摩亚 Samoa	685	WST	0.399	4	0.195	166	阿皮亚 Apia	萨摩亚语 Samoan
大洋洲 Oceania	瓦努阿图 Vanuatu	678	VUV	16.954	3	0.27	167	维拉港、桑托岛 Port Vila, Santo	英语 English
大洋洲 Oceania	汤加 Tonga	675	TOP	0.354	5	0.107	172	努库阿洛法、内亚富 Nukualofa, Neiafu	英语 English
大洋洲 Oceania	密克罗尼西亚 Micronesia	691	USD $	0.154	2	0.1049	174	波纳佩、埃贝耶 Pohnpei, Ebeye	英语 English
大洋洲 Oceania	马绍尔群岛 Marshall Island	692	USD $	0.154	4	0.053	176	马朱罗环礁 Majuro	英语 English
大洋洲 Oceania	基里巴斯 Kiribati	686	AUD A$	0.201	4	0.1143	177	塔拉瓦岛、巴纳巴岛 Tarawa, Banaba	英语 English

续表

洲 Continent	国家或地区 Country or Area	A	B	C	D	E	F	G	H
大洋洲 Oceania	图瓦卢 Tuvalu	688	TVD	0.207	4	0.011	178	富纳富提 Funafuti	英语 English
大洋洲 Oceania	帕劳 Palau	680	USD $	0.154	1	0.0215	175	科罗尔 Koror	帕劳语 Palau
非洲 Africa	尼日利亚 Nigeria	234	NGN	54.752	7	185.9	25	哈科特港、拉各斯 Port Harcourt, Lagos	英语 English
非洲 Africa	埃及 Egypt	20	EGP	2.728	6	91.69	79	苏伊士港、苏科纳 Port Suez,Sokhna	阿拉伯语 Arbic
非洲 Africa	南非 South Africa	27	ZAR	2.07	6	55.9	34	开普敦、比勒陀利亚 Cape Town,Pretoria	英语 English
非洲 Africa	阿尔及利亚 Algeria	213	DZD	17.92	7	40.61	52	阿尔及尔、阿尔泽 Algiers, Arzew	阿拉伯语 Arbic
非洲 Africa	摩洛哥 Morocco	212	MAD	1.44	8	35.27	57	地中海丹吉尔港、 阿加迪尔 Port Tangier Mediterranee, Agadir	阿拉伯语 Arbic
非洲 Africa	安哥拉 Angola	244	AOA	37.571	7	28.81	58	卡宾达、洛比托 Cabinda,Lobito	葡萄牙语 Portuguese
非洲 Africa	苏丹 Sudan	249	SDG	2.74	5	39.58	63	苏丹港 Port Sudan	阿拉伯语 Arbic
非洲 Africa	埃塞尔比亚 Ethiopia	251	ETB	4.16	5	102.4	65		阿姆哈拉语 Amharic
非洲 Africa	肯尼亚 Kenya	254	KES	15.401	5	48.46	66	蒙巴萨、内罗毕 Mombasa, Nairobi	斯瓦希里语 Kiswahili
非洲 Africa	坦桑尼亚 Tanzania	255	TZS	346.86	5	55.57	80	姆特瓦拉、桑给巴尔 Mtwara,Zanzibar	斯瓦希里语 Kiswahili

洲 Continent	国家或地区 Country or Area	A	B	C	D	E	F	G	H
非洲 Africa	加纳 Ghana	233	GHS	0.732	8	28.21	83	阿克拉、特马 Accra，Tema	英语 English
非洲 Africa	突尼斯 Tunisia	216	TND	0.397	7	36.89	85	突尼斯、斯法克斯 Tunis，Safx	阿拉伯语 Arbic
非洲 Africa	科特迪瓦 Coate d'Ivoire	225	XOF	84.96	8	23.7	88	阿比让、圣佩德罗 Abidjan， San pedro，ci	法语 French
非洲 Africa	利比亚 Libya	218	LYD	0.208	6	6.29	89	的黎波里、图卜鲁格 Tripoli，Tobruk	阿拉伯语 Arbic
非洲 Africa	喀麦隆 Cameroon	237	XAF	85.65	7	23.44	91	杜阿拉 Douala	法语 French
非洲 Africa	乌干达 Uganda	256	UGX	591.42	5	41.49	95	坎帕拉 Kampala	英语 English
非洲 Africa	赞比亚 Zambia	260	ZMW	1.5	6	16.591	97	恩多拉、基特韦 Ndola，Kitwe	英语 English
非洲 Africa	莫桑比克 Mozambique	258	MZN	0.1527	6	28.829	100	克利马内、马普托 Quelimane， Maputo	葡萄牙语 Portuguese
非洲 Africa	塞内加尔 Senegal	221	XOF	84.96	8	15.41	108	达喀尔 Dakar	法语 French
非洲 Africa	加蓬 Gabon	241	XAF	85.65	7	1.98	110	利伯维尔、谦蒂尔港 Libreville， Port gentil	法语 French
非洲 Africa	津巴布韦 Zimbabwe	263	ZAR	2.072	6	16.15	112	布拉瓦约、哈拉雷 Bulawayo， Harare	英语 English
非洲 Africa	纳米比亚 Namibia	264	NAD	2.06	7	2.48	113	卢德立次、鲸湾港 Luderitz， Walvis Bay	英语 English
非洲 Africa	乍得 Chad	235	XAF	85.65	7	14.5	115	恩贾梅纳 NDjamena	英语 English

洲 Continent	国家或地区 Country or Area	A	B	C	D	E	F	G	H
非洲 Africa	博茨瓦纳 Botswana	267	BWP	1.579	6	2.251	117	弗朗西斯敦、 哈博罗内 Francistown, Gaborone	英语 English
非洲 Africa	布基纳法索 Burkina Faso	226	XOF	84.96	8	18.65	119	瓦加杜古 Ouagadougou	法语 French
非洲 Africa	马里 Mali	223	XOF	84.96	8	17.99	122	巴马科、卡伊 Bamako, Kayes	法语 French
非洲 Africa	毛里求斯 Mauritius	230	MUR	5.293	4	1.26	123	路易港 Port Louis	英语 English
非洲 Africa	刚果 Republic of the Congo	242	XAF	85.65	7	5.126	124	布拉柴维尔、黑角 Brazzaville, Pointe Noire	法语 French
非洲 Africa	赤道几内亚 Equatorial Guinea	240	XAF	85.65	7	1.22	127	巴塔、马拉博 Bata, Malabo	西班牙语 Spanish
非洲 Africa	卢旺达 Rwanda	250	RWF	129.91	6	11.92	129	基加利 Kigali	卢旺达语 Kinyarwanda
非洲 Africa	马达加斯加 Madagascar	261	MGA	500.11	5	24.89	130	图阿马西纳、 塔马塔夫 Toamasina, Tamatave	马达加斯加语 Malagasy
非洲 Africa	尼日尔 Niger	227	XOF	84.96	7	20.67	135	加亚、尼亚美 Gaya, Niamgy	法语 French
非洲 Africa	贝宁 Benin	229	XOF	84.96	7	10.87	133	科托努 Cotonou	法语 French
非洲 Africa	几内亚 Guinea	224	GNF	1376.9	8	12.396	137	科纳克里 Conakry	法语 French
非洲 Africa	马拉维 Malawi	265	MWK	109.12	6	18.092	139	布兰太尔、利隆圭 Blantyre, Lilongwe	英语 English

洲 Continent	国家或地区 Country or Area	A	B	C	D	E	F	G	H
非洲 Africa	厄立特里亚 Eritrea	291	ERN	2.29	5	6.7	141	马萨瓦、阿萨布 Massawa， Assab	英语 English
非洲 Africa	毛里塔尼亚 Mauritania	222	MRO	54.29	8	4.3	142	努瓦迪布、 努瓦克肖特 Nouadhibou， Nouakchott	阿拉伯语 Arbic
非洲 Africa	塞拉利昂 Sierra Leone	232	SLL	1220.5	8	7.4	144	弗里敦 Freetown	英语 English
非洲 Africa	多哥 Togo	228	XOF	84.96	8	7.61	145	洛美 Lome	法语 French
非洲 Africa	斯威士兰 Swaziland	268	SZL	2.065	6	1.34	147	马扎巴 Matsapha	英语 English
非洲 Africa	布隆迪 Burundi	257	BIF	267.79	6	10.52	149	布琼布拉 Bujumbura	基隆迪语 Kirundi
非洲 Africa	利比里亚 Liberia	231	LRD	22.52	8	4.61	152	蒙罗维亚 Monrovia	英语 English
非洲 Africa	莱索托 Lesotho	266	LSL	2.08	6	2.2	153	马塞卢 Maseru	英语 English
非洲 Africa	吉布提 Djibouti	253	DJF	27.17	5	0.942	154	吉布提 Djibouti	法语 French
非洲 Africa	中非 Central African	236	XAF	85.65	7	4.59	155	班吉 Bangui	法语 French
非洲 Africa	佛得角 Cape Verde	238	CVE	14.41	9	0.54	157	明德卢港、普拉亚 Mindelo，Praia	葡萄牙语 Portuguese
非洲 Africa	塞舌尔 Seychelles	248	SCR	2.053	4	0.0947	160	维多利亚港 Victoria，sc	克里奥尔语 Creole
非洲 Africa	几内亚比绍 Guinea-Bissau	245	XOF	84.96	8	1.82	163	比绍 Bissau	葡萄牙语 Portuguese

续表

洲 Continent	国家或地区 Country or Area	A	B	C	D	E	F	G	H
非洲 Africa	冈比亚 Gambia	220	GMD	7.15	8	2.04	169	班珠尔 Banjul	英语 English
非洲 Africa	科摩罗 Comoros	269	KMF	64.49	5	0.8	170	莫罗尼 Moroni	科摩罗 Comorian

4. Abbreviations for International Trade 外贸跟单常用英文缩略语

a accepted 承兑

AA Auditing Administration（中国）审计署

AAA 最佳等级

abs. abstract 摘要

a/c，A/C account 账户、账目

a/c，A/C account current 往来账户、活期存款账户

A&C addenda and corrigenda 补遗和勘误

Acc. acceptance or accepted 承兑

Accrd. Int accrued interest 应计利息

Acct. account 账户、账目

Acct. ccountant 会计师、会计员

Acct. accounting 会计、会计学

Acct.No. account number 账户编号、账号

Acct.Tit. account title 账户名称、会计科目

ACN air consignment 航空托运单

a/c no. account number 账户编号、账号

Acpt. acceptance or accepted 承兑

A/CS Pay. accounts payable 应付账款

A/CS Rec. accounts receivable 应收账款

ACT advance corporation tax 预扣公司税

TSP total suspended particle 总空中悬浮物(污染指标)

TST test 检查，检测

TT Testamentary Trust 遗嘱信托

TT，T/T telegraphic transfer 电汇

T.T.B. telegraphic transfer bought 买入电汇

T.T.S. telegraphic transfer sold 卖出电汇

TTY teletypewriter 电报打字员

TU Trade Union 工会,职工协会

Tue，Tues Tuesday 星期二

TV terminal value；television 最终价值；电视

TW transit warehouse 转口仓库

TWI training within industry 业内训练

txt. text 课文,电文,正文

Ty. territory 领土,(推销员的)推销区域

T&E Card travel and entertainment card 旅行和娱乐信用卡

T&H temperature and humidity 温度和湿度

T&M time and material 时间和材料

T/C time charter 定期租船,计时租船

t/km tonper kilometer 吨/千米

TOP Trade Opportunities Program (美国)贸易机会计划

T.O.P. turn over，please 请翻转

TPM total productive maintenance 总生产维修(护)制

TPND theft，pilerage，and non-delivery 偷窃及不能送达险

tpo telephoto 电传照片,传真

TQ tariff quota 关税配额

T.Q.，t.q. tale quale (拉丁)按现状,现状条件

TQC total quality control 全面质量控制

TR telegram restante；trust receipt 留交电报；信托收据

T.R. tons registered (船舶)注册吨位

Tr. transfer 过户,转让

traditio symbolia (拉丁)象征性交费

Tranche CD certificate of deposit 份额存单

trans translated 译本

treas treasurer 会计,出纳,库管,司库

Trip. triplicate 一式三份中的一份

Triple A 3A 3A 级,最佳债券评级

TRS terminal receiving system 港外待运仓收货制度

TRT Trademark Registration Treaty 商标注册条约

t.f. till forbid 直到取消为止

tgm. telegram 电报

three T's type，terms，technique 交易三要素,即交易类型,交易条件,销售技术

thro.，thru. through 经由,通过

Thu. Thursday 星期四

TIP to insure promptness 确保迅速

TIR carnet Transports Internationaux Routier (法国)国际公路运输证

tks. thanks 致谢,感谢

tkt ticket 票

TL time loan; total loss; trade-last 定期贷款;总损失;最后交易

TLO, T.L.O. total lossdisabled_by_dv__only=free from/of all average 全损赔偿险

TLX telex=teleprinter/teletypewriter exchange 电传

TM trademark 商标

TM telegram with multiple addresses 分送电报

TMA Terminal Market Association 最终市场协会

TMO telegraph money order 电汇单

TN treasury note 国库券

TNC transnational/multinational company 跨国公司

TOD time of delivery 发货时间

Tonn. tonnage 吨位(数)

TC telegraph collation 校对电报

T.C. traveler's check 旅行支票

TCI trade credit insurance 贸易信用保险

TCIC technical credit insurance consultants 技术信用保险顾问

TCM traditional Chinese medicine 中国传统医学,中医

TD time deposit 定期存款

TD Treasury Department (美国)财政部

TDA Trade Development Authority 贸易发展当局

TDC technical development corporation 技术开发公司

TDC Trade Development Council (香港)贸易发展局

TDR Treasury Deposit Receipt 国库券存据

Tech technical 技术的

Tel. telephone number 电话号码

telecom telecommunications 通信

temp temperature; temporary (secretary) 温度;临时(秘书)

TESSA Tax Exempt Special Savings Account 免税特别储蓄账户

TEU twenty-foot-equipment unit (货柜、集装箱)20 英尺当量单位

TF trade finance 贸易融资

t time; temperature 时间;温度

T. ton; tare 吨;包装重量,皮重

TA telegraphic address=cable address 电报挂号

TA total asset 全部资产,资产

TA trade acceptance 商业承兑票据

TA transfer agent 过户转账代理人

TAB tax anticipation bill (美国)预期抵税国库券

TACPF tied aid capital projects fund 援助联系的资本项目基金

TAF tied aid financing 援助性融资

TAL traffic and accident loss（保险）交通和意外事故损失

TAT truck-air-truck 陆空联运

TB treasury bond, treasury bill 国库券,国库债券

T.B. trial balance 试算表

t.b.a. to be advised；to be agreed；to be announced；to be arranged 待通知;待同意;待宣布；待安排

t.b.d. to be determined 待（决定）

TBD policy to be declared policy 预保单,待报保险单

TBL through bill of lading 联运提单,直达提单

TBV trust borrower vehicle 信托借款人工具（公司）

TBW Thompson Bankwatch, a rating agent 托马逊银行评估公司

TC tariff circular 关税通报

SPF spare parts financing 零部件融资

SPQR small profits, quick returns 薄利多销

SPS special purpose securities 特设证券

Sq. square 平方;结清

SRM standard repair manual 标准维修手册

SRP Salary Reduction Plan 薪水折扣计划

SRT Spousal Remainder Trust 配偶幸存者信托

ss semis, one half 一半

SS social security 社会福利

ST short term 短期

ST special treatment（listed stock）特别措施（对有问题的上市股票）

St. Dft. sight draft 即期汇票

STB special tax bond 特别税债务

STIP short-term insurance policy 短期保险单

sub. subscription；substitute 订阅,签署,捐助;代替

Sun. Sunday 星期日

sund. sundries 杂货,杂费

sup. supply 供应,供货

SIC Standard Industrial Classification 标准产业分类

SIP structured insurance products 结构保险产品

SITC Standard International Trade Classification 国际贸易标准分类

sk. sack 袋,包

SKD separate knock-known 部分散件

SLC standby LC 备用信用证

SMA special miscellaneous account 特别杂项账户

SMEs small and medium-sized enterprises 中小型企业

SMI Swiss Market Index 瑞士市场指数

SML security market line 证券市场线

SMTP supplemental medium term policy 辅助中期保险

SN stock number 股票编号

Snafu Situation Normal, All Fouled Up 情况还是一样,只是都乱了

SOE state-owned enterprises 国有企业

SOF State Ownership Fund 国家所有权基金

sola sola bill, sola draft, sola of exchange（拉丁）单张汇票

sov. sovereign 1 英镑＝20 先令

SOYD sum of the year's digits method 年数加总折旧法

spec. specification 规格;尺寸

SEA Single European Act《单一欧洲法案》

SEAF Stock Exchange Automatic Exchange Facility 股票交易所自动交易措施

SEATO Southeast Asia Treaty Organization 东南亚公约组织

sec. second(ary); secretary 第二,次级;秘书

sect. section 部分

Sen. senator 参议院

Sept. September 九月

SET selective employment tax 单一税率工资税

sextuplicate （文件）一式六份中的一份

SEC special economic zone 经济特区

SF sinking fund 偿债基金

Sfr Swiss Frank 瑞士法郎

SFS Summary Financial Statements 财务报表概要

sgd. signed 已签署

SHEX Sundays and holidays excepted 星期日和假日除外

SHINC Sundays and holidays included 星期日和假日包括在内

shpd. shipped 已装运

shpg. shipping 正装运

shpt. shipment 装运,船货

SI Statutory Instrument; System of Units 有效立法;国际量制

SBLI Savings Bank Life Insurance 储蓄银行人寿保险

SBN Standard Book Number 标准图书号

SC sales contract 销售合同

sc. scilicet namely 即

SC supplier credit 卖方信贷

SCF supplier credit finance 卖方信贷融资

Sch schilling（奥地利）先令

SCIRR special CIRR 特别商业参考利率

SCL security characteristic line 证券特征线

SCORE special claim on residual equity 对剩余财产净值的特别要求权

SD standard deduction 标准扣除额

SDB special district bond 特区债券

SDBL sight draft，bill of lading attached 即期汇票，附带提货单

SDH synchronous digital hierarchy 同步数字系统

SDR straight discount rate 直线贴现率

SDRs special drawing rights 特别提款权

SE shareholders' equity 股东产权

SE Stock Exchange 股票交易所

SA semi-annual payment 半年支付

SA South Africa 南非

SAA special arbitrage account 特别套作账户

SAB special assessment bond 特别估价债券

sae stamped addressed envelope 已贴邮票、写好地址的信封

SAFE State Administration of Foreign Exchange 国家外汇管理局

SAIC State Administration for Industry and Commerce（中国）国家工商行政管理局

SAP Statement of Auditing Procedure《审计程序汇编》

SAR Special Administrative Region 特别行政区

SAS Statement of Auditing Standard《审计准则汇编》

SASE self-addressed stamped envelope 邮资已付有回邮地址的信封

SAT（China）State Administration of Taxation（中国）国家税务局

SATCOM satellite communication 卫星通信

SB short bill 短期国库券；短期汇票

SB sales book；saving bond；savings bank 售货簿；储蓄债券；储蓄银行

SBC Swiss Bank Corp. 瑞士银行公司

SBIC Small Business Investment Corporation 小企业投资公司

SBIP small business insurance policy 小型企业保险单

RPM resale price maintenance 零售价格维持措施(计划)

rpt. repeat 重复

RRP Reverse Repurchase Agreement ？毓盒焯？ br />RSL rate sensitive liability 利率敏感性债务

RSVP please reply 请回复

RT Royalty Trust 特权信托

RTM registered trade mark 注册商标

Rto ratio 比率

RTO round trip operation 往返作业

RTS rate of technical substitution 技术替代率

RTW right to work 工作权利

RUF revolving underwriting facility 循环式包销安排

RYL referring to your letter 参照你方来信

RYT referring to your telex 参照你方电传

S no option offered 无期权出售

S split or stock divided 拆股或股息

S signed 已签字

s second；shilling 秒;第二;先令

REVOLVER revolving letter of credit 循环信用证

REWR read and write 读和写

RIEs recognized investment exchanges 认可的投资交易(所)

Rl roll 卷

RLB restricted license bank 有限制牌照银行

RM remittance 汇款

rm room 房间

RMB RENMINBI 人民币,中国货币

RMS Royal Mail Steamer 皇家邮轮

RMSD Royal Mail Special Delivery 皇家邮政专递

RMT Rail and Maritime Transport Union 铁路海运联盟

ROA return on asset 资产回报率

ROC return on capital 资本收益率

ROE return on equity 股本回报率

ROI return on investment 投资收益

ROP registered option principal 记名期权本金

ro-ro roll-on/roll-off vessel 滚装船

ROS return on sales 销售收益率

RPB Recognized Professional Body 认可职业(投资)机构

RPI retail price index 零售物价指数

R&T rail and truck 铁路及卡车运输

R&W rail and water 铁路及水路运输

R/A refer to acceptor 洽询(汇票)承兑人

R/D refer to drawer (银行)洽询出票人

RB regular budget 经常预算

RCA relative comparative advantage 相对比较优势

RCMM registered competitive market maker 注册的竞争市场自营商

rcvd. received 已收到

r.d. running days＝consecutive days 连续日

RDTC registered deposit taking company 注册接受存款公司

Re. subject 主题

re. with reference to 关于

RECEIVED B/L received for shipment bill of lading 待装云提单

REER real effective exchange rate 实效汇率

ref. referee；reference；refer(red) 仲裁者；裁判；参考；呈递

REO real estate owned 拥有的不动产

REP import replacement 进口替代

REP Office representative office 代办处,代表处

REPO，repu，RP Repurchase Agreement 再回购协议

req. requisition 要货单,请求

q. quarto 四开,四开本

Q. quantity 数量

QB qualified buyers 合格的购买者

QC quality control 质量控制

QI quarterly index 季度指数

qr. quarter 四分之一,一刻钟

QT questioned trade 有问题交易

QTIB Qualified Terminal Interest Property Trust 附带可终止权益的财产信托

quad. quadruplicate 一式四份中的一份

quotn. quotation 报价

q.v. quod vide (which see) 参阅

q.y. query 查核

R option not traded 没有进行交易的期权

R. response；registered；return 答复；已注册；收益

r. rate；rupee；ruble 比率；卢比；卢布

RAD research and development 研究和开发

RAM diverse annuity mortgage 逆向年金抵押

RAN revenue anticipation note 收入预期债券

R&A rail and air 铁路及航空运输

R&D research and development 研究与开发

PF project finance 项目融资

PFD preferred stock 优先股

pk peck 配克(1/4 蒲式耳)

PMO postal money order 邮政汇票

P.O.C. port of call 寄航港,停靠地

P.O.D. place of delivery 交货地点

P.O.D. port of destination；port of discharge 目的港；卸货港

P.O.R. payable on receipt 货到付款

P.P. payback period（投资的）回收期

P.P.I. policy proof of interest 凭保证单证明的保险利益

POE port of entry 报关港口

POP advertising point-of-purchase advertising 购物点广告

POR pay on return 收益

PR payment received 付款收讫

PS postscript 又及

PV par value；present value 面值；现值

P&A professional and administrative 职业的和管理的

P&I clause protection and indemnity clause 保障与赔偿条款

P&L profit and loss 盈亏，损益

P/A payment of arrival 货到付款

P/C price catalog；price current 价格目录；现行价格

P/E price/earning 市盈率

P/H pier-to-house 从码头到仓库

P/N promissory note 期票，本票

P/P posted price（股票等）的牌价

PAC put and call 卖出和买入期权

pat. patent 专利

PAYE pay as you earn 所得税预扣法

PAYE pay as you enter 进入时支付

PBT profit before taxation 税前利润

pc piece；prices 片，块；价格

pcl. parcel 包裹

pd paid 已付

per pro. per procurationem（拉丁）由……代理

o.m.s. output per manshift 每人每班产量

O.P.old price 原价格

O.P.open policy 不定额保险单

opp opposite 对方

opt. optional 可选择的

ord. ordinary 普通的

OS out of stock 无现货

O/s outstanding 未清偿、未收回的

O.T. overtime 加班

OTC over-the -counter market 市场外交易市场

OVA overhead variance analysis 间接费用差异分析

OW offer wanted 寻购启示

OWE optimum working efficiency 最佳工作效率

oz ounce(s) 盎司

ozws. otherwise 否则

p penny; pence; per 便士;每

P paid this year 该年(红利)已付

p. pint 品托(1/8 加仑)

P.A. particular average; power of attorney 单独海损;委托书

P.A. personal account; private account 个人账户、私人账户

p.a., per ann. per annum 每年

OB other budgetary 其他预算

O.B. ordinary business 普通业务

O.B. (O/B) order book 订货簿

OB/OS index overbought/oversold index 超买超卖指数

OBV on-balance volume 持平数量法

o. c. over charge 收费过多

OC open cover 预约保险

o/d, o. d.,(O. D.) overdrawn 透支

OD overdraft 透支

O/d on demand 见票即付

O.E. (o. e.) omission excepted 遗漏除外

O.F. ocean freight 海运费

OFC open for cover 预约保险

O.G. ordinary goods 中等品

O.G.L. Open General License 不限额进口许可证

OI original issue 原始发行

OII overseas investment insurance 海外投资保险

ok. all correct 全部正确

N.S.F. (NSF) no sufficient fund 存款不足

NSF check no sufficient fund check 存款不足支票

nt. wt. net weight 净重

NTA net tangible assets 有形资产净值

NTBs non-tariffs barriers 非关税壁垒

ntl no time lost 立即

NTS not to scale 不按比例

NU name unknown 无名

N.W. net worth 净值

NWC net working capital 净流动资本

NX not exceeding 不超过

N.Y. net yield 净收益

NZ$ New Zealand dollar 新西兰元

o order 订单

o. (O.) offer 发盘、报价

OA open account 赊账、往来账

o/a on account of 记入……账户

o.a. overall 全面的、综合的

OAAS operational accounting and analysis system 经营会计分析制

NM no marks 无标记

N. N. no name 无签名

NNP net national product 国民生产净值

NO. (no.) number 编号、号数

no a/c no account 无此账户

NOP net open position 净开头寸

NOW a/c negotiable order of withdrawal 可转让存单账户

N/P net profit 净利

NP no protest 免作拒付证书

N. P. notes payable 应付票据

NPC nominal protection coefficient 名义保护系数

NPL non-performing loan 不良贷款

NPV method net present value method 净现值法

N.Q.A. net quick assets 速动资产净额

NQB no qualified bidders 无合格投标人

NR no rated (信用)未分等级

N/R no responsibility 无责任

N.R. notes receivable 应收票据

nego. negotiate 谈判

N.E.S. not elsewhere specified 未另作说明

net. p. net proceeds 净收入

N/F no fund 无存款

NFD no fixed date 无固定日期

NFS not for sale 非卖品

N.G. net gain 纯收益

NH not held 不追索委托

N.I. net income 净收益

N.I. net interest 净利息

NIAT net income after tax 税后净收益

NIFO next in, first out 次进先出法

nil nothing 无

NIM net interest margin 净息差

NIT negative income tax 负所得税

N.L. net loss 净损失

NL no load 无佣金

n.m. nautical mile 海里

n. net 净值

N.A. net assets 净资产

n. a not available 暂缺

N. A. non-acceptance 不承兑

NA not applicable 不可行

N. B. nota bene 注意

NC no charge 免费

N/C net capital 净资本

n. d. no date 无日期

N. D. net debt 净债务

n. d. non-delivery 未能到达

ND next day delivery 第二天交割

NDA net domestic asset 国内资产净值

N.E. net earnings 净收益

n. e. no effects 无效

n. e. not enough 不足

negb. negotiable 可转让的、可流通的

Neg. Inst., N. I. negotiable instruments 流通票据

MOS management operating system 经营管理制度

Mos. months 月

MP market price 市价

M/P months after payment 付款后……月

MPC marginal propensity to consume 边际消费倾向

Mrge.(mtg.) mortgage 抵押

MRJ materials requisition journal 领料日记账

MRO maintenance, repair and operation 维护、修理及操作

MRP manufacturer's recommended price 厂商推荐价格

MRP material requirement planning 原料需求计划

MRP monthly report of progress 进度月报

MRR maintenance, repair and replace 维护、修理和更换

months of sight 见票后……月

msg. message 留言

MT medium term 中期

M/T mail transfer 信汇

mthly monthly 每月

MTI medium-term insurance 中期保险

MTN medium-term note 中期票据

MTU metric unit 米制单位

mg. milligram 毫克

M/I marine insurance 海险

micro one millionth part 百万分之一

min. minimum 最低值、最小量

MIP monthly investment plan 月度投资计划

Mk. mark 马克

mks. marks 商标

mkt. market 市场

MLR minimum lending rate 最低贷款利率

MLTG medium-and-long-term guarantee 中长期担保

M. M. money market 货币市场

mm. millimeter 毫米

MMDA money market deposit account 货币市场存款账户

MMI major market index 主要市场指数

MNC multinational corporation 跨(多)国公司

MNE multinational enterprise 跨国公司

MO（M. O.）money order 汇票

mo. month 月

M/C marginal credit 信贷限额

m/c metallic currency 金属货币

MCA mutual currency account 共同货币账户

MCP mixed credit program 混合信贷计划

M/d months after deposit 出票后……月

M. D. maturity date 到期日

M. D.（M/D）memorandum of deposit 存款(放)单

M. D. malicious damage 恶意损坏

mdse. merchandise 商品

MEI marginal efficiency of investment 投资的边际效率

mem. memorandum 备忘录

MERM multilateral exchange rate model 多边汇率模型

M. F. mutual funds 共同基金

MF mezzanine financing 过渡融资

mfg. manufacturing 制造的

MFN most favoured nations 最惠国

mfrs. manufacturers 制造商

《纺织品经营与贸易》(职业教育"现代纺织技术"专业国家教学资源库建设子项目)